Tasting Grace

A Mentoring-in-the-Kitchen Bible Study

Leah Adams & Jan Morton

Warner Press, Inc

Warner Press and Warner Press logo are trademarks of Warner Press, Inc.

Tasting Grace: A Mentoring-in-the-Kitchen Bible Study
Written by Leah Adams and Jan Morton

Requests for information should be sent to:
Warner Press Inc
1201 East Fifth Street
P.O. Box 2499
Anderson, IN 46012
www.warnerpress.org

Editors: Karen Rhodes, Robin Fogle
Cover and layout: Curtis Corzine

ISBN: 9781593178802

Printed in USA

FOREWORD

BIBLE STUDY

TASTING GRACE RECIPES

LEADERS' GUIDE /EVENT PLANNER

AFTERWORD

"I remember clearly thinking that real relationships don't develop online. I liked social media but thought we'd all be wise to accept it for what it was even at its best: a community 10 miles wide and a quarter inch deep. It seemed like a great place to cheer people on but, in my estimation, authentic ministry could not take root in virtual soil. Boy was I wrong. God used no one to prove me wrong more than Jan Morton. We met and began interacting in an online community of fabulous women with all sorts of hopes and dreams and troubles and needs much like our own. Jan and I found ourselves tag-teaming in the community, one encouraging this sister in Christ, the other encouraging that one. Soon many joined us in this symbiotic sisterhood and, lo and behold, something supernatural happened. God worked the wonder of true community and ministry.

I fell in love with those women and none more than Jan. Our common bonds are almost endless. We are the same age, married almost the same number of years, we love our adult children to no end and have the privilege of grandparenting kids around the same age. Raised on hymns, sermons, Sunday school and missions, the strongest bond we share is Jesus. Her path was not nearly as messy as mine but she declares to me often that she needed Him just as desperately.

That same Jesus put a very similar call on our lives. We love to serve women in His glorious name. Even though I became a believer in authentic ministry online, I still believe that it is most effective face-to-face. Shoulder-to-shoulder. Elbow-to-elbow. What can replace the soundtrack of true affection or unearth the same empathy as the sight of tears?

I am a huge fan of the Leah and Jan approach to mentoring women. Kitchen counters become sacred spaces and holy conversations take place over the clack and clatter of pans and dishes. The women laugh, lament life's painful bent, and boast in Jesus and His gracious sufficiency. Godly counsel stirs up over savory chopped garlic, and discipleship rises warm from the oven with the scents of cinnamon.

I'm not sure a person can find a better combination for tasting and seeing that the Lord is good. This concept for bringing women together is divine brilliance. It is the treasured update of what many women took for granted for centuries. We need each other. And we are often at our best after enjoying Jesus together. I am honored to invite you to savor this book like a fine, home-cooked meal. And stick around for dessert."

Beth Moore

INTRODUCTION

Sharing Cooking, Jesus, and Life in the Kitchen

God seems to love taking the ordinary and fashioning it into something extraordinary. The ordinary becomes the extraordinary in the hands of the Master. Jan and I believe we are seeing God do this very thing in the mentoring-in-the-kitchen ministry He has ordained for us. Few things are more ordinary than preparing meals.

Many women learned to cook while standing beside their mother or grandmother. We watched, listened, learned and enjoyed time spent in the kitchen with other women. In today's fast-paced, fast food society, there is a generation of young women who have not had the joy of being mentored in the kitchen by another woman. We believe this has left a void in the lives and hearts of many women. Out of this void was born *Tasting Grace: A Mentoring-in-the-Kitchen Ministry*.

In the book you hold in your hand, you will find food to feed the heart and the tummy. *Tasting Grace: A Mentoring-in-the-Kitchen Bible Study* represents our desire to connect the generations through face-to-face mentoring and cooking. It incorporates two things in which we take great delight: studying Scripture and cooking.

Tasting Grace is a Bible study first and an event-planning guide. You do not have to plan a *Tasting Grace* event to fully engage in the Bible study portion of this book, but should you desire to, we have provided you with the planning tools you will need.

Tasting Grace for Individual or Group Bible Study Experience
Perhaps you have a desire to become a mentor in the kitchen and you have picked up this book to learn how we organize, prepare for, and host our events. Wonderful! We have given you our entire process in this book, broken down into weekly segments that will help you organize your thoughts, prepare a list of potential participants, issue an invitation, and set the stage for you to host a single *Tasting Grace* event in your kitchen, just as we have.

We hope you, and those God places in your path, are blessed by *Tasting Grace*—the study and the event.

Come, friend, taste the grace!

BIBLE STUDY
Week 1– Mentors in the Word

In our time in the Word this week, we will look at the topic of mentoring as we visit with a few mentors who set a godly example for us. Paul, Moses, Aquila and Priscilla, and Jesus have much to teach us about mentoring. The goal is for your time in Scripture each day to be about 15 minutes long and to offer a spiritual challenge for your heart.

DAY 1 - PAUL AND TITUS

Mentoring. The word can be quite intimidating, can't it? It sounds as though it requires special skills and training. Many women hear the word and immediately think, "Oh, I could never be a mentor. I'm not spiritual enough."

The truth is that mentoring does not require any special skills. Rather, it requires a special heart that is tender toward others and longs to sow into their lives. That's all it takes. Any time one person helps another person learn a job or life skill, mentoring is taking place.

Consider the apostle Paul. Now *there* is a mentor. We will spend some time shadowing Paul over the course of the next four weeks, but today I want to narrow our focus to the classic words from the pen of Paul on this topic of mentoring.

Please turn in your Bible to the tiny, power-packed book of Titus. This little book in a nutshell is Paul's encouragement to Titus to teach sound doctrine that will lead to good works. In Titus chapter 2 we find Paul mentoring Titus so that Titus can mentor his church.

The whole Paul and Titus thing reminds me of the children's song we used to sing entitled "Dem Bones."
> *"The toe bone's connected to the foot bone, The foot bone's connected*
> *to the ankle bone, The ankle bone's connected to the leg bone…."*

Oops, sorry, I got carried away. Jan's husband is a minister of music, so we were rocking out here. Anyway, where was I? Yes, the mentoring of Titus by Paul. Paul mentored Titus. Titus was to mentor the older men and women in his church. The older folks were to mentor the younger folks. Let's take a look at Paul's words to Titus.

Please turn in your Bible to **Titus 2:1**. What does Paul encourage Titus to teach?

_____

_____

_____

I bet you are asking, "What is sound doctrine?" Well, Paul is going to tell us.

Slowly and carefully read **Titus 2:2-5**. In each category below, please list what Titus is to teach to each group. I will give you an example from the first category.

OLDER MEN ARE TO BE:

sober-minded, dignified, self-controlled, sound in faith, in love, and in steadfastness.

OLDER WOMEN ARE TO BE:

_____

_____

_____

_____

YOUNGER WOMEN ARE TO:

_____

_____

_____

_____

I think it will be time well spent if we take just a moment to dig into a couple of the words that Paul uses here.

Titus is to encourage the older women to be reverent in the way they live and not to be slanderers. Now, I don't think there is a single one of us who wakes up in the morning and thinks, "I want to be an irreverent slanderer today." *Anyone?* No, I didn't think so.

So, why would Paul instruct Titus to even address these issues? It helps to understand the original words that Paul would have used. The Greek word for reverent implies that these women should conduct themselves as if God were right beside them, watching their every move. They should never do anything that would cause embarrassment if Jesus showed up at that moment. The truth is that Jesus is watching our every move, so we should always engage in reverent, sacred behavior.

When we think of the word "slander," we think of saying things about another person that may or may not be true, but saying it in a way that intentionally causes harm. The Greek word used in verse 3 for slanderers is…hold onto your hats….*diabolos*. This, my friends, is not a compliment. Paul is telling Titus to flat out tell the older women that they do not need to be "she-devils"! Ouch!! I've known a few. I've been one.

I'm sorry to add insult to injury, but the Greek word *diabolos* is the word that is used to reference the devil as the chief-demon-in-charge. It is also the word that was applied to Judas by Jesus when he betrayed our Lord. This is no small matter. We are not to be she-devils, stirring up trouble and speaking hurt toward others.

Finally, the older women are to encourage the younger women to be pure. The Greek word used here means that the younger women are to live with integrity. It is specifically speaking of sexual integrity. They are to be sexually pure, whether single or married. How much our world needs a little purity today!

The last few words of Titus 2:5 should shake us to the very core of our beings, sisters. Every single one of us at one time or another has been a "younger woman." Even if you are 75 years old today, you could be considered a younger woman in some area of life. So what I am about to say is pertinent to every woman.

The final few words of **Titus 2:5** give us the reason for mentoring. Write them here:

_____

_____

_____

_____

It makes me shiver to think of how many times my behavior has caused another person to revile, malign, or look down on the gospel. I have heard those who do not know Christ, in response to the actions of a Christian, say, "If that is what being a Christian is all about, I don't want it." When the actions of a Christian cause an unbeliever to revile or despise the gospel, substantial damage is done.

Our actions should point others to Christ, not drive them away from Him. We must live godly lives so that those who do not know Christ might come to know Him as Savior and Lord.

What's Cooking? How did the Lord speak to you today?

_____

_____

_____

_____

_____

_____

_____

_____

_____

_____

_____

_____

_____

DAY 2 – Moses and Joshua

If the requirements for being a good mentor included perfect behavior, I would be in a peck of trouble. With a track record like mine, it astounds me that God would use me as a mentor. I made poor choices in so many areas of my life in my younger days, yet in God's grace and mercy I have found forgiveness and restoration. Thankfully, there is no waste in God's economy. He can take our poor choices and turn them into amazing mentoring opportunities if we are willing to be used for His glory.

Moses was a man who made a few poor choices. He was a murderer and a rock-smacker, yet God used him to mentor the man who would ultimately lead Israel into the Promised Land.

Let's drop in on Moses and Joshua today.

Please turn to **Numbers 11:28** and record what we are told about the relationship between Moses and Joshua. Be sure to note how long this relationship had been present.

_____

_____

_____

Read **Exodus 17:9-14** and answer the following:

What did Moses instruct Joshua to do in verse 9? _____

_____

In verse 10 we are told that Joshua did as Moses instructed. A good mentor is trustworthy. Moses was sending Joshua into battle where he could be killed. Based on what you read about Joshua in verse 10, did he trust Moses, his mentor? _____

_____

In verse 14, God tells Moses to write down the account of what happened as a memorial in a book. What was Moses to do with that account that he wrote down?

_____

_____

This was a teachable moment! Mentors have teachable moments with their mentees. Whether it is talking about the consequences of a behavior or tossing out ingredients in a recipe gone bad and starting over, capturing teachable moments are crucial in a mentoring relationship.

In **Deuteronomy 1:38**, we find God instructing Moses to do something that is a vital part of mentoring. What did God tell Moses to do for Joshua? _____

_____

Encouragement. Oh, how we need that in our lives. There is a precious plenty to **dis**-courage us in the world today. We need to be encouraged in our walks with Christ, our parenting, our marriages, our school lives, and our jobs.

A godly mentor is an encourager.

I want you see one final portrait from the lives of Moses and Joshua. Turn to **Joshua 1:1-9**, read it and answer the following questions.

What is Joshua called in these verses? _____

In order to be someone's aide, you have to be in close proximity to them, observing them and hearing from them. Joshua had walked with Moses for many years. In those years, Moses had mentored Joshua. He had encouraged Joshua. He had taught Joshua.

Now, Moses is gone and it is Joshua's time to lead. Because Moses had been a faithful mentor, and Joshua a faithful student, God promised Joshua something in verses 5 and 9. Please take a moment and write out these two verses, focusing specifically on the last half of each verse.

_____

_____

_____

_____

_____

_____

_____

Friend, God makes the same promise to all who are His children through the blood of Jesus. He will never leave or forsake you. He will be with you wherever you go. Moses' faithfulness to mentor Joshua was now bearing fruit. Joshua would go forth with the blessing of God on his life and work.

Your faithfulness to mentor and be mentored will reap untold benefits for you and those around you. Lean into mentoring, dear one. It is God-ordained and God-blessed.

WHAT'S COOKING? How did God speak to you today?

_____

_____

_____

_____

_____

DAY 3 – Aquila, Priscilla, and Apollos

Today we wander into the book of Acts and contemplate the lives of three followers of Jesus. One is a man named Apollos that the Bible describes as eloquent and competent in the Scriptures. The other two are a husband and wife team named Aquila and Priscilla. They are tentmakers, traveling companions of Paul, and leaders in a house church that meets in their home. Because of their shared faith in Christ, the lives of Apollos, Aquila, and Priscilla intersect in Ephesus. They provide the perfect opportunity for us to ponder a character trait that is crucial in mentoring relationships.

Let's see if you can discern what trait I am talking about by reading the story of how these three met. Please turn to **Acts 18:24-28** and read it carefully, then answer the questions below.

List here every word or phrase that describes Apollos in these verses:

_____

_____

_____

_____

_____

_____

_____

Apollos sounds like a well-educated man who was confident and capable, doesn't he? He was teaching the Scriptures accurately and with boldness. This could describe many pastors and teachers of the Word down through the ages, as well as today.

Enter Aquila and Priscilla. Return to Acts 18:24-28 and note the actions of this husband and wife. _____

_____

_____

_____

I hope by now you are starting to get a sense of the character trait that I want us to talk about today. It is humility. A lack of pride. A teachable spirit. Humility is crucial in ministry and in life.

All three of these individuals exemplified humility. Apollos was a confident, capable teacher of the Scriptures, who taught with boldness. Yet, when Aquila and Priscilla took him aside and taught him a bit more about Jesus and the way of God, he did not respond in pride. There is no evidence that he became defensive toward this couple. As a result of the humility and teachable spirit of Apollos, verses 27 and 28 tell us that he was powerfully used by Christ in Achaia. If he had "bucked up," as my daddy used to say, and had not been receptive to the teaching of Aquila and Priscilla, it is likely that the Lord would not have used him to spread the good news of the gospel.

Likewise, Aquila and Priscilla exhibited humility in their approach to Apollos. As leaders in the church, they could have called him out publicly on his teaching, and in doing so, alienated him. Instead, they took him aside privately and sought to teach him a more excellent way. This couple mentored Apollos out of humility, and Apollos responded in the same way.

Just to make certain that we understand how much God loves humility and hates pride, let take a look at a few verses dealing with these traits. Look up the following verses and note what the Scripture says about humility and pride.

Proverbs 6:16-17 _____
_____
_____
_____

Proverbs 16:18 _____
_____
_____
_____

Micah 6:8 _____
_____
_____
_____

God expects us to walk humbly before Him and other people. Pride and lack of a teachable spirit will destroy mentoring relationships. I encourage you to ask the Lord to reveal any pride that is hidden in your heart and to help you walk in humility with Him.

WHAT'S COOKING? How did God speak to you today?

_____
_____
_____
_____
_____
_____
_____
_____

DAY 4 – Jesus: On Pride, Humility and Children

Effective communicators know the importance of repetition. God used repetition, well….repeatedly…because He knew that we needed to be reminded and reminded and reminded of important concepts. Today, I want to employ the same tactic and cover a concept that we examined yesterday. The concept of humility is *THAT* important, so jump on board and let's go.

Let's listen in as Jesus mentors His disciples in the art of humility. Every time I read this story, I am embarrassed for the disciples. I think, "How could they have been so ridiculous?" Then, I remember times that I have been just as prideful. The truth is that none of us are immune to prideful thoughts. It's just that they don't always spew forth from our mouths and become part of the biblical record!

Please turn in your Bible to **Mark 9. Read verses 33–35 and answer the following questions.**

What question did Jesus ask the disciples in verse 33? _____
_____
_____
_____

What answer did they give? _____
_____

How did Jesus respond to their silence in verse 35? _____
_____
_____
_____

Ouch! Those men probably felt like the holy hand of God had smacked them upside of the head. I don't know about you, but I think I would have been looking for a table to crawl beneath. Oh, how prideful we can be!

When Jesus told His disciples that they must be willing to be last in order to be first, the word He used for "last" means dead last, at the very end. Likewise, the word used for servant implies not only a humble position, but also a spirit of gratefulness in that humble position. This is the same word that is used for our modern term "deacon" in the church. Deacons are to be humble, grateful servants in the body of Christ.

A mentor *must* be humble. A mentor *must* have the heart of a servant when they deal with other people. As mentors interact with their mentees, the heart of a servant should be evident in a thousand ways. When it comes to humility, mentors are to lead and teach by example.

We have talked for two days about humility and having a servant's heart. We have heard Jesus tell His disciples what is needed in order to be first in His kingdom. Now, let's finish up today by pondering a statement that sent me to knees the first time I heard it. Are you ready?

The real test of humility is how you react when someone treats you like a servant.

Give that a minute to settle in all over. It is easy (and prideful) to think, "Of course, I'm humble." And, perhaps you are. The true test of my humility…of your humility…is how we react when someone treats us as if we are his or her servant or slave. I don't know about you, but I fail the humility test when I get treated like I am someone's slave.

Jesus would say to me and to you, "Sister, if you want to be considered great by Me, you have to be willing to be treated like a slave—to be last in the eyes of the world." I'm not talking about letting someone abuse you, or use you as a doormat. What I am talking about is being willing to serve others out of humility. Jesus set the example of the last being first, and the first becoming last. Let's follow His example.

WHAT'S COOKING? How did God speak to you today?

_____

_____

_____

_____

_____

_____

_____

_____

_____

_____

_____

_____

_____

_____

_____

_____

_____

_____

_____

DAY 5 – JESUS TEACHES HIS DISCIPLES

Have you ever washed the feet of another person? Have you ever had your own feet washed by someone else? Both washing the feet of another person and having your own feet washed are incredibly humbling experiences. In John 13, Jesus mentored His disciples in this act of humility and servanthood. Let's visit with Him for a moment.

Turn in your Bible and read **John 13:1-17**.

Picture it. God the Son, the One who hung the stars in the universe, knelt down and washed the dirty, smelly feet of humanity.

In Jesus' day the feet were the filthiest part of a person because the primary mode of transportation was either walking or riding on the back of a horse or donkey. Most people walked, so their feet were constantly caked with either dust or mud.

A good hostess would always provide water to her guests for the washing of their feet. Today in our study time, we see Jesus not only provide that water, but also kneel down and wash those feet.

Please answer the following questions based on the John 13 passage.

Read verse 1. How did Jesus feel about His people, His "own"?

_____

_____

_____

I am crazy about the way the NIV phrases this concept. It says, "Having loved his own who were in the world, he now showed them the full extent of his love."

Washing the feet of these men would be the first in a series of actions by Jesus that would offer stunning evidence of His love for all people. Let's take a peek at the words of Jesus to the disciples after He finished washing their feet.

Write **John 13:14** here:

_____

_____

_____

_____

_____

In this verse Jesus tells His disciples that they now have the responsibility to do as He did. He had been their Teacher, Lord, and mentor in spiritual things. Now, they needed to act on what they had learned. He would be leaving them shortly, and they would be left as His representatives in the world. You and I, friends, are left as His representatives in our world.

Jesus was not just telling the disciples that washing the feet of those around them would be a good idea. No! The word that he used for should or ought can be better understood as a command with a bit of fatherly guilt tossed in. He had washed their feet. Now, they were indebted to Him for what He had done, and would do, for them to the extent that the only way to even begin to repay Him would be to do as He had done.

Was Jesus telling these men to go out and wash the feet of every person they met? Is that what He is saying to you and me? Well, maybe, but maybe not. There are a thousand ways that you and I can wash the feet of another person.

We can:
- Deliver a meal when someone is sick or has lost a loved one
- Mow the grass of an elderly neighbor
- Offer to babysit so a stressed-out mom can have an hour to herself
- Pay the power bill for a family who cannot pay their own bill
- Speak a kind word to the down and out
- Spend an hour visiting the nursing home
- Serve soup in a homeless shelter
- Support a missionary with your finances and prayers
- Lead a Bible study
- Mentor a middle school girl or boy

Every time we reach out to another person in the name and love of Jesus we are washing their feet. It would be awesome if you could find a way to participate in a literal washing of the feet of another person. Perhaps you could wash the feet of the other people in this study group. Perhaps you could wash the feet of your friend, your neighbor, your pastor. Take some time today to pray about how you can wash the feet of other people, both literally and symbolically.

WHAT'S COOKING? How did God speak to you today?

_____

_____

_____

_____

_____

_____

_____

_____

_____

_____

Bible Study
Week 2 – Invitations in Scripture

This week we will spend our time examining invitations in Scripture. We will begin with the invitation God issued to Abraham to leave and go. At first blush, it sounds like a command, but we will see that it was truly an invitation to deeper faith. The rest of the week will be spent letting the invitations of Jesus teach us. I hope you are blessed by this week of study in the Scriptures.

Day 1 – Leave and Go

Sometimes an invitation is a no-brainer. For example, "Would you like to come with me for an ice cream?'" would be a decision requiring less than a nano-second of consideration for me. *Ice cream? I'm there. May I have butter pecan, please?*

Other invitations, however, might not be so easy to accept. Case in point: **Genesis 12:1-4** where we find God issuing an invitation to Abram, aka. Abraham. Please read these verses in your Bible now.

Allow me to give you a bit of backstory. Abram was a man who lived in Ur and also in Haran, which was in modern day Iraq and Turkey. His folks, as we say in the South, were not church-going people. In fact, we are told in Joshua 24:2 that his family was an idol worshipping clan. We are not told if they *had* worshipped idols or *were still* worshipping idols in Abram's lifetime. I guess it doesn't really matter. What does matter is that at some point, Abram had an encounter with Jehovah God that birthed a faith in him that is still talked about today.

One day, God came calling and issued Abram an invitation to pack up everything he owned and hit the road. In the space below, write out what God invited Abram to do in **Genesis 12:1**. Remember, invitations can seem like commands, and it is only in hindsight that we realize it was truly an invitation.

_____

_____

_____

_____

_____

_____

This is more than an invitation to an ice cream party. This is an invitation to faith. When God invites a man to leave everything he knows and loves, you can be sure that God has big plans for that man.

The Scripture does not give us much in the way of details between verse 1 and verse 4. Abram was told to leave his family. His family! Brothers, sisters, parents, aunts, uncles….the fabric of his life was to be left behind.

He was also to leave his security. Whatever his livelihood was, he was told to leave that behind. How would he support his family as they traveled? Would he be able to do the same type of work in the new land? So many unanswered questions.

Ultimately, God took Abram hundreds of miles away from Ur and Haran. This was not an easy journey, but one that was walked out step-by-step, on foot or camelback. Surely, at some point in the long journey, Abram paused to question whether he had made the right decision to obey God's call.

The stunning thing about this story is found in verse 4 of Genesis 12. We are told that when God issued the invitation, Abram went.

> **No questions.**
>
> **No bargaining with God.**
>
> **No arguing.**
>
> **No procrastinating.**

The man just packed up and went. His wife, too.

That, friends, is RADICAL OBEDIENCE. It would have been tempting for Abram to bargain with God. He could have said, "May I just offer you a few sacrifices. Please do not make me leave everything that I know and love."

How often does God ask you to do something, and you just do it? Without questioning. Without reasoning it through to make it make sense. *(Often God's requests do not make sense, in the human realm.)* No questions asked; you just do it.

That kind of radical obedience is not commonplace in our world. Why is that? Could it be we do not really trust God enough to be radically obedient?

Let's finish with one more verse. Please write out **1 Samuel 15:22** in the space below.

_____

_____

_____

_____

_____

_____

God desires our obedience. Period. There is blessing for obedience. Are you willing to obey whatever He asks of you?

WHAT'S COOKING? How did God speak to you today?

DAY TWO - Follow Me

Invitations. They carry with them equal parts excitement and trepidation. Take, for instance, an invitation from that cute guy to the fall ball or the office Christmas party. You have been trying to catch his eye for weeks, but he never seemed interested. Then, one day he stops by your desk and begins to talk to you.

You do your best to remain calm on the outside, but your insides are like a quivering bowl of Jell-o™. A few days later he casually asks if you would like to go with him to the party. You are not sure whether to say "yes" first or throw up from excitement.

Once you catch your breath and tell him that you would love to go to the party with him, the trepidation and anxiety set in. What will you wear? How will you wear your hair? And what in the world will you talk about with him?

Excitement, coupled with anxiety.

Have you ever wondered if those men that Jesus called to follow Him felt that odd mixture of emotions? Certainly, they had no idea what following Jesus would truly cost. Let's visit with Matthew, also called Levi, as he hears the invitation from Jesus to follow Him.

Please read **Mark 2:13-14** and answer the following questions.

Where does verse 13 tell us that Jesus was teaching at this time?

_____

Where was Matthew when Jesus saw him?

_____

What did Jesus say to Matthew?

_____

What was Matthew's response?

_____

_____

Luke 5:28 adds words to what we already know from Mark 2:14. What are these two words?

_____

Matthew was a tax collector. You and I have little appreciation for the connotation of those two words, tax collector. In Jesus' day the tax collectors, while Jewish, were usually in cahoots with the Pharisees and with Rome. They were known to be thieves who skimmed the top money for themselves. They did this by charging more in taxes than the citizens actually owed, then pocketing the extra for their own greedy gain.

Needless to say, Matthew would not have won a "citizen of the year'" award. Yet, Jesus sees something in Matthew that causes Him to call the tax collector into His inner circle. The fact that Matthew left everything to follow Jesus is huge. In spite of being hated, Matthew was likely quite well off financially. Saying "yes" to Jesus meant that suddenly Matthew had no job and no income. His only friends, up to this point, were probably other tax collectors. Now, he was walking away from job, money, and friends to follow this itinerant preacher named Jesus.

Sometimes following Jesus may cost us dearly. It may cost us our comfort, security, income, or family. Although there was no way that Matthew could know the consequences of his decision to follow Jesus, he followed without question or doubt. He left everything and followed Jesus.

Have you wholeheartedly followed Jesus? Are you convinced that following and obeying Jesus is worth whatever you have to leave? For those who follow Him, Jesus promises eternal blessings. Follow hard after Him!

WHAT'S COOKING? How did God speak to you today?

_____
_____
_____
_____
_____
_____
_____
_____
_____
_____
_____
_____
_____
_____
_____
_____
_____
_____
_____
_____
_____
_____
_____
_____

DAY 3 – Take Up Your Cross

The Cross. Today, we wear it as jewelry around our necks and hang it on our walls as decoration. The cross has become a common and accepted symbol of religious belief.

It was not so in Jesus' day. People of that day would have been horrified to think that a cross would be considered as jewelry or decoration. You see, the cross was a horrendous instrument of Roman torture—the worst death sentence one could receive. To be crucified meant that death would be excruciatingly painful and slow. Often the one being crucified was scourged prior to the crucifixion, so as to speed up the dying process from blood loss. Sometimes the one hanging on the cross died so slowly that those in charge of the crucifixion ended up doing things to hasten the person's death so as be able to move on to something else.

Being condemned to a Roman cross was the worst way imaginable to die. So, for Jesus to speak of the cross in the months prior to His death would, likely, be horrifying to His listeners. Let's join them and see what He has to tell us about the cross.

Please read **Luke 9:23-24.**

Jesus issued two invitations in verse 23 for anyone who wanted to follow Him. What were the two things that Christ followers must do?

1. _____

2. _____

Jesus had just foretold His own death in the moments prior to these verses. We have no indication, however, that He specified the means by which He would die. So, for Him to tell His followers that they need to take up their cross and follow Him daily would have caused much angst among the faithful. Only common criminals died on a cross. Why in the world would Jesus use that kind of language to describe following Him?

Jesus knew that in order to follow Him, we would need to allow Him to live in and through us. Our flesh wants its own way and it wants the easy way, but Jesus' way is not always easy, nor is it always the way we would choose.

Take a moment and in the space below write out some ways that Christians today might deny themselves and take up their cross to follow Jesus. I'll give you one to start you out.

Choose television programs, movies, books and music that are pleasing to God rather than those that may be popular, but do not honor God.

_____

_____

_____

_____

Now, look up the following Scriptures and note how they are pertinent to denying oneself and taking up the cross to follow Christ.

Galatians 2:20

_____

_____

Galatians 6:7-9

_____

_____

Philippians 4:8-9

_____

_____

Jesus never promised that responding to His invitation to follow Him would be easy or painless. In fact, He promised that doing so would cost the follower. Yet, He also promised blessings for those who were obedient to the call.

Are you following Him wholeheartedly today? Have you made the intentional choice to deny your flesh, take up the cross and follow Him? If not, why not? Choose wisely, friend. You will never regret following Jesus.

WHAT'S COOKING? How did God speak to you today?

_____

_____

_____

_____

_____

_____

_____

_____

_____

_____

_____

_____

_____

_____

_____

_____

DAY 4 – WEARY OF RULES AND LAWS? NEED REST? COME!

Rules and laws are a part of everyone's life. No matter where you live, there are laws you must obey and rules to be followed. Some make sense; others, not so much!

Speed limit: 65 miles per hour

Employees MUST wash hands before returning to work!

Income Tax filing deadline: April 15th

"The footing or anchorage for scaffolds shall be sound, rigid, and capable of carrying the maximum intended load without settling or displacement. Unstable objects such as barrels, boxes, loose brick, or concrete blocks shall not be used to support scaffolds or planks." US Dept of Labor OSHA website

"This statute prohibits an executive branch employee from receiving any legal fees, partnership share, bonuses, or any other form of compensation derived from representational services of others in matters before the executive branch or the courts (when the United States is a party or has a direct and substantial interest). This bar applies to representations while the person is an executive branch employee, regardless of whether he or she receives the funds during or after Government service." US Office of Government Ethics website

In one state, bingo games are prohibited from lasting more than five hours. *Really??*

In yet another state it is illegal to drive with an uncaged bear. *Seriously, who does that?*

Rules and laws govern almost everything we do.

This was also the case in the day in which Jesus lived. The 10 Commandments had morphed into more than six hundred laws to be followed in order to please the Pharisees and leaders. Some of the laws made sense, while others were hard to figure out.

Jesus and His disciples ran afoul of the Pharisees on more than one occasion as they ministered in the regions of Galilee and Jerusalem. Many times the Pharisees tried to catch Jesus breaking the law of the Sabbath.

Jesus knew that it was impossible to keep every law on the Jewish books. He knew it because He was the Great Lawgiver, and He had a purpose for those unkeepable laws.

Write **Romans 5:20** in the space below.

_____

_____

_____

_____

In Matthew 11, we find Jesus addressing the legalism of keeping the law that the Pharisees placed on the people. Before we go there, lets make sure we understand what the term "legalism" means. Legalism, as we are using the term today, means strict adherence to the letter of the law with no exceptions for grace or mercy.

Please read **Matthew 11:28-30** and answer the following questions:

To whom does Jesus issue this invitation?

_____

What does He promise to give them?

_____

For those who come, Jesus encourages them to take something from Him. What is it?

_____

How does Jesus describe His yoke?

_____

_____

The Greek word that Jesus uses for yoke conveys the idea of a pair of oxen held together by a yoke. The oxen work in tandem, both pulling the load. Jesus tells us that if we take on His yoke, He will be linked with us, helping us walk through this life. If we try to shoulder the load of life alone, we will be weighed down, weary, and frustrated. But, if we allow Jesus to link up with us in the yoke, He takes much of our burden and makes it His. Suddenly our yoke becomes lighter.

Do you have a burden that you need to cast on Jesus? A yoke that needs the broad shoulders of Jesus joined/harnessed with your shoulders? Take Jesus up on His invitation to come and take on His yoke.

WHAT'S COOKING? How did God speak to you today?

_____

_____

_____

_____

_____

_____

_____

DAY 5 – WALKING ON THE WATER

When was the last time you walked on water? *Never?* Me either, unless you count the glass of water I spilled on my kitchen floor. Water walking doesn't happen much today, so why in the world would God place the story of Peter walking on the water in the Holy Scriptures?

Let's hop in the boat with Peter and company and see what we can learn today.

Please read **Matthew 14:22-33.**

Jesus and the disciples have been busy ministering and preaching in the region of Galilee. Crowds followed them everywhere, wanting to hear what He had to say. The sick and lame wanted to be healed. The Pharisees wanted to catch Jesus breaking the law. It seemed there was never a quiet moment to be had.

On this particular night, Jesus sends the twelve across the Sea of Galilee to wait on Him while He spends time with the Father. Jesus knew something they did not know. He knew that Peter and company were about to get in a mess of trouble on the sea. He also knew that He had a purpose for that trouble.

Do you ever get so busy that you lose your focus? Does life crowd in and crowd out your time with Jesus? Is your own pride ever your undoing? Does the tyranny of the urgent control you… *ever*?

Jesus had called the disciples to a good and godly work…a work of sharing the gospel to a lost and dying people. These twelve men worked hard, following Jesus, assisting Him, learning from Him, serving Him. They had seen amazing miracles of healing and casting out of demons. Could it be that they had become more enamored with the show than the Savior? Had they come to rely more on the position they were in than the Person of Jesus? Remember, this was the same group who argued about who would sit on Jesus' right hand in the kingdom!

What did Peter ask of Jesus in **Matthew 14:28**?

_____

_____

_____

_____

If it is You? Apparently ghost stories were a big thing in that day, too, for the Bible says that the disciples thought they might be seeing a ghost.

Peter asked Jesus to command him to come to Him on the water. When Jesus issued the command, Peter got down out of the boat and walked on the water. If there had been cameras in those days, don't you know Peter would have been taking a selfie!

Peter made one mistake, however. Please write out verse 30 in the space below.

_____

_____

_____

_____

_____

At some point he took his eyes off of Jesus and put them on his circumstances. He looked around at the wind and waves and forgot about Jesus, who gave him the invitation and power to walk on the water. Suddenly, the water that had been beneath his feet was engulfing his body. He was going under because he took his eyes off of the one who commands the wind and the waves.

Jesus knows when we are fully focused on Him and when we have our eyes on our circumstances. Sometimes, you and I can be like Peter and need a refocusing of our gaze. That is when He will orchestrate circumstances that will force us to look to Him, and Him only.

Perhaps you are in a place in your life right now where the wind and waves are threatening to engulf you. It is time to take **Hebrews 12:2** seriously. What does this verse tell us to do?

_____

_____

_____

_____

Are you ready? Are you willing to fix your eyes on Jesus instead of your circumstances? Cry out to Him, friend. He will save you.

WHAT'S COOKING? How did God speak to you today?

_____

_____

_____

_____

_____

_____

_____

_____

_____

_____

BIBLE STUDY
Week 3 – Preparing Our Hearts for Jesus' Calling

Our time in the Scripture this week examines ways that we can, and must, prepare our hearts for the work that Jesus longs to do in them. We must have clean hearts, submitted hearts, and dedicated hearts that are ready and willing for Him to work in and through.

This week may require something more than just reading and writing down answers. It may require some heart work that can be uncomfortable at times. Do it anyway! It is worth it. Your relationship with Jesus will grow exponentially as a result of what takes place this week.

DAY 1 – PREPARED HEARTS

If you have walked with Jesus more than a pair of days, you may have learned that the heart He can use best is the prepared heart, the submitted heart. Jesus is an all-or-nothing kind of guy. He wants complete access to a totally surrendered heart.

Many of us want Jesus to work in our lives, but we are not willing to throw open every single door in our heart and invite Him to move in. When we are saved, we ask Jesus to come into our heart to live. Once He has saved us, then the process of cleaning us up begins. That is called sanctification, and it is not for sissies.

Read **Psalm 139:1-24**. Verses 1-5 tell us that God knows all about us. Note here the words and phrases that confirm that God is intimately acquainted with us.

_____

_____

_____

_____

_____

_____

_____

When you invite company into your home, you clean house in order to prepare for them. You scrub the toilets, dust the furniture, vacuum the floors, and change the sheets on the bed. You want things to be neat, clean, and inviting when your guests arrive.

If you are like me, however, you always have one or two rooms that are off-limits to guests. Those are what I like to call the junk rooms. The junk room is where everything gets tossed that you need to get out of sight but don't have a particular place to put it. The junk room is where we hide our stuff, our junk.

Our hearts are often no different. We invite Jesus in to be our Savior. Often, though, we put up a "keep out" sign on the door of our heart's junk room. Jesus can have all of us, except what is in our junk room. There are a few things in there that we hold back. Things like pet sins, past hurts, and pervasive shame. We think that if we open the door to that room, Jesus could never forgive us for that thing. If we open the door to that room, He will take away the pet sin that we hang on to so tightly. If we open the door to the junk room, Jesus will make us forgive the person that hurt us so terribly. We could never open the door and give Jesus access to *that* room.

The truth is, when we place a "keep out" sign on any door in our heart, we tell Jesus that we do not *really* want Him to Savior *and Lord*. We want Him to allow us to be comfortable in our sin and shame and hurt. We want to be saved from the fires of hell, but we do not want Him to do the painful work of completely cleaning out our hearts.

Oh, if only we realized that the cleaning out Jesus does is for our good. His cleaning relieves us of our anxieties and our shame. It frees us from the stronghold of sin and places us smack in the center of His will for our lives.

Please return to Psalm 139 and write out verses 23 and 24 in the space below.

_____

_____

_____

_____

_____

_____

Now, if you truly want to know the peace and joy that Jesus offers when you allow Him to clean you up, please take a moment and turn those two verses into a prayer. Ask Him to search your heart and point out anything in your heart and life that does not please Him. When He does, and He will, be willing to immediately give Him access to that. Confess it to Him, and allow Him to take it away. Then, friend, you will find the peace that comes from a clean and pure heart.

🍲 WHAT'S COOKING? How did God speak to you today?

_____

_____

_____

_____

_____

_____

_____

_____

DAY 2 – CLEAN HEARTS

Today's study time may seem like a repeat of yesterday, but I want us to explore another passage that speaks to the issue of recognizing sin and allowing Jesus to clean it out of our hearts.

Please read **Psalm 51:1-17** and describe in your own words what this passage is about.

_____

_____

_____

_____

_____

_____

_____

In 2 Samuel 11 we find that David, the mighty King of Israel, had sinned in hideous ways. He had committed adultery, deception, and murder. It seemed that he had gotten away with it, until Nathan the prophet shows up at David's door.

Using a parable, Nathan shines a laser beam into the heart of the king and exposes the ugly sins committed and hidden by David. Exposed and guilty, David has two choices: He can continue his deception and denial of the sin, or he can go to God in repentance and ask for forgiveness. Wisely, he does the latter.

When David goes to God, he has two choices. He can tell God that he will do his best to clean up his act, or He can allow God to clean him up. Again, he wisely chooses the latter.

You and I live in a bootstrap world. We are taught from a young age that when we fall we should dust ourselves off and pick ourselves up by our bootstraps. Work harder to look and be better. The only problem is that God's doesn't work like that. There is not a single thing you and I can do to clean ourselves up from our sin. Only God can truly clean us up.

In the following verses from Psalm 51, write out the words or phrases that David uses to ask God to clean him up from his sin. There may be more than one in some verses. I will give you the first one.

Verse 1 – _Blot out my transgressions_____

Verse 2 – _____

Verse 7 – _____

Verse 9 – _____

Verse 10 – _____

Verse 12 - _____

David knew that the only way he could be free of the guilt of his sins was to take them to God in humility and repentance, allowing God to do the cleaning of his heart.

I want us to look at one more bit of wisdom in this passage. Remember I said that David thought he had gotten away with his sin? David may have thought he had gotten away with it, but it was eating him up inside.

In Psalm 51:3 David confesses that, even though no one else knew about his sin, he knew. Every morning when he arose, his sin greeted him. Every evening when he went to bed, he tossed and turned over what he had done. In verse 8 he admits that his joy had disappeared, and he felt as if his bones were being crushed by the weight of his guilt. That is what sin does to us. It destroys our joy, our health, and our peace.

Is there sin in your life that has not been confessed to God? Are you suffering the effects of hidden sin? I want to encourage you to run straight to God with it. Confess it before Him, and find peace and joy once again.

WHAT'S COOKING? How did God speak to you today?

_____
_____
_____
_____
_____
_____
_____
_____
_____
_____
_____
_____
_____
_____
_____
_____
_____
_____
_____
_____

DAY 3 - All In

Several years ago God began placing a specific set of verses before me. Romans 12:1-2 began showing up everywhere I looked. I read them in my Bible study time. I heard them on the radio. I head them in the pastor's sermon. I seriously expected to see them scrawled on a bathroom wall somewhere. God was relentless in making sure those verses were front and center in my mind and heart for almost two years.

Has that ever happened to you? It seems God knows that you and I, His precious dust-bunnies, need repetition and reinforcement of key concepts in Scripture. He certainly knows that I do.

Needless to say, I memorized those verses and took them very seriously. Even today, many years later, I pray these verses over my life on a regular basis.

Today, I want us to consider those two verses. Please take a moment and turn to **Romans 12:1-2**. Read the passage twice, and then write it in the space below.

_____

_____

_____

_____

_____

_____

_____

_____

Let us look at three commands given in these verses that I believe will revolutionize our lives if we will take them seriously:

- Offer your body as a living sacrifice
- Do not conform to the pattern of the world
- Be transformed by the renewing of your mind

Offer your body as a living sacrifice.

In the Old Testament when something was sacrificed it was placed on an altar and killed. Our bodies house our mind, will, and emotions, and are the earthly tents in which we journey through this life. Thus, our bodies are the place where sin affects us. Paul encourages us to offer our bodies (figuratively) as a sacrifice to God. I will typically do this by flinging wide my arms, looking into the heavens, and saying to God, "I'm yours. Every bit of me. Body, soul, and spirit. Mind, will, and emotions. I offer myself to You, Lord. Jesus, live through me."

It has been said the problem with living sacrifices is that they tend to crawl off the altar. *Can I get an Amen?* We give ourselves to God, then take back the part that we do not want Him to have. We simply need to give Him all of us, even if it is painful to do so. He knows how to mold us into the pattern of Jesus.

Do not conform to the pattern of the world.

The world is the domain of Satan. It is where he is allowed, for a time, to exercise power. The world bears the mark of Satan. It is riddled with sin and shame. We conform to the world when we walk in the ways of the world.

Galatians 5:17-21 gives us a picture of what we look like if we conform to the world. Circle the words that describe a person who conforms to the world based on this passage.

Peaceful	Sexually immoral	Pure	Selfish	Kind
Jealous	Envious	Faithful	Drunk	Patient
Stirs up trouble	Self-controlled	Joyous	Raging	Loving

As Christians, we must conform to the image of Jesus, rather than the image of the world. It is only when we have Jesus living inside of us, and we are submitted to Him, that we will conform to His image.

Be transformed by the renewing of your mind.

There is only one way to be transformed by the renewing of your mind, friend. Allow me to take you to two passages that will show you how to do this. Note what you find in these passages that causes mind transformation and renewal.

Hebrews 4:12

_____

_____

Psalm 119:9

_____

_____

_____

Becoming a student of Scripture is the key to renewing your mind and transforming your life once you accept Jesus as your Lord and Savior.

So, are you ready to go all in? Offer your body as a living sacrifice to Jesus, cease conforming to the world's ways, and transform your mind through Scripture. If you will regularly do these three things, your life will be pleasing to God, and you will leave an amazing legacy for those who circle your life.

WHAT'S COOKING? How did God speak to you today?

DAY 4 – It's All About Focus

To be the best at anything, one has to be able to focus on the goal. It is true in sports, in life, and in faith. The best golfer in the world does not allow himself to be distracted by other sports. He does not try to excel at golf and baseball and tennis. He focuses solely on golf and diligently pursues excellence in the sport.

The story is told of a fifth century monk named Telemachus. In his travels, he came to Rome and happened into the gladiatorial arena where a contest was taking place. He was so revolted by the brutality and inhumanity of the slaughter, he jumped into the arena and cried out three times, "In the name of Christ, forebear!"

The Roman crowd was so enraged by Telemachus' actions that they stoned him to death on the spot; however, Honorius the emperor was a Christian. He was so impressed by the selflessness and Christian focus of Telemachus that he issued an edict throughout the Roman territory, banning the gladiatorial contests.

Focus. Because Telemachus was focused on Christ, he sacrificed his life in an effort to save the lives of the gladiators. So it is with our faith. Please read **Hebrews 12:1-2** and answer the following questions.

In verse 1 we are told that we, as Christ-followers, are surrounded by something. What surrounds us?

_____

_____

Each of us is involved in a race…a race of faith that begins when we accept Christ and ends when we take our last breath on this earth. How are we encouraged to run this race in verse 1?

_____

_____

Verse 2 gives us the key to running the faith race with perseverance. What is that key?

_____

_____

_____

When Jesus came to this earth, He came with one purpose. He was born to die. Period. Yes, Jesus preached the gospel of salvation. He healed the sick and raised the dead. He cast out demons from the possessed. Jesus worked in many ways while He was on earth. Yet, the reason He came was to die, and He never allowed His focus to stray from that purpose.

While His disciples preached the gospel, healed the sick, and cast out demons, there was no other person who could die to provide salvation. That job belonged to Jesus, and Him alone. His focus—His purpose—was salvation.

While Jesus died to provide the way of salvation, you and I are the ones in this age who shine the light of salvation for a world enshrouded in darkness. We must keep our eyes focused on Jesus in order to accomplish the task before us.

There is so much to distract us from Jesus. Work, family, friends, finances, problems, health, and much more. Yet, in the midst of it all, if we keep our gaze fixed firmly on Him, we will know joy, peace, and contentment. We will be lights that shine brightly for Him, and others will be drawn to Jesus.

So, eyes on Jesus, friend. Fix your focus and find Him faithful.

WHAT'S COOKING? How did God speak to you today?

DAY 5 – THOUGHTS

This week we have asked God to search our hearts and create cleanness and holiness in them. We have offered our bodies to God as living sacrifices and fixed our focus on Jesus. What is next?

Turn with me to **Philippians 4:4-8**. Read this passage then answer the following questions.

In verses 4-6, we are encouraged to do several things. List them here.

_____

_____

_____

_____

_____

_____

Verse 8 instructs the Christian how to think. There are 8 things that Paul tells us to think upon. What are they? List them here.

1. _____

2. _____

3. _____

4. _____

5. _____

6. _____

7. _____

8. _____

The Greek word used by Paul for *think* in this verse means to take an inventory of, reason, conclude. Paul is encouraging us to make these kinds of thoughts the norm, rather than the exception.

Now, to the right of each of the above listed words from Philippians 4:8, please list the word that is the antonym, or opposite of that word. For example, the antonym, or opposite of true is false. If you need to consult a dictionary, please do so.

Finally, make an honest assessment of your thought patterns. In the course of a day, what percentage of your thoughts fall into the categories of true, noble, right, pure, lovely, admirable, excellent, and praiseworthy?

Oh my! I don't know about you, but for me, that is a sobering, convicting question. I've got some work to do on my thought-life. How about you?

I want to take you to two more verses that will help with this exercise of thinking on things that are excellent.

Hebrews 3:1 tells us where to focus our thoughts so that they are proved excellent. Note the answer here.

_____

_____

Now, let's end with a prayer that will help us be victorious in this effort of thinking on praise-worthy things. Please write out **Psalm 19:14** in the space below. Once you have written it, turn it into a prayer for your life.

_____

_____

_____

_____

_____

When we ask the Lord to make the words of our mouths and the meditations, or thoughts, of our hearts acceptable to Him, He will do it.

WHAT'S COOKING? How did God speak to you today?

_____

_____

_____

_____

_____

_____

_____

_____

_____

_____

_____

_____

_____

_____

_____

BIBLE STUDY
Week 4 – Living and Looking Like Christ in a Desperate World

This week in our Bible study time, we will join the apostle Paul and ask him to become our mentor. As our older brother in the faith, Paul has much to teach us about living and looking like Christ to a world that so desperately needs to know Him. Our time with Paul will require much of us—humility, introspection, and the willingness to allow the Word of God to change us.

Our time in the Word holds great promise for life and heart change if we will hold loosely the things of this world and our own desires. Paul knows a lot about the walk of faith, and we will be wise to hear and heed his words.

DAY ONE – Not Ashamed

Ashamed. The word dredges up a host of feelings, and most of them are not pleasant. There is the "I am so ashamed that I did _____." When our own actions bring shame down on our heads, the hurt is real and palpable. If only we could turn back the clock and make a different choice. If only….

Then there is the "I am ashamed of you" that is aimed squarely at us and leaves gaping wounds in our heart. A person who is disappointed with our actions or words often flings this one out because they want us to feel the immense depth of their disappointment.

The apostle Paul knew that Christians throughout time would have the opportunity to feel ashamed on many occasions. Observant Jews who chose to follow Jesus were the source of shame to their fellow devout Jews. Disciples of Jesus, both Jew and Gentile, would be ridiculed and persecuted throughout history for following Jesus. Being a follower of Jesus Christ has never been about taking the easy path. Jesus reminded us of this in John 16.

Fill in the blank from a portion of **John 16:33**.

In this world, _____ _____ _____ _____…

As our mentor in the faith, Paul offers us a powerful statement from his own life that should serve to encourage us on our journey, even as we wrestle with the trials of our day.

Please write out **Romans 1:16** in the space below.

_____

_____

_____

_____

_____

_____

Friends, there is really no way to dance around this verse. It is a clarion call to courage and steadfastness in our faith. We live in a time where we, as Christ-followers, are increasingly singled out because of our faith and labeled with less than flattering labels.

Intolerant
> *Bigoted*
>> *Homophobic*
>>> *Inflexible*
>>>> *Judgmental*
>>>>> *Unloving*

I think you get the picture. While those who do not know Jesus often affix these labels to Christians, sometimes they are tossed toward a Christian by a Christian. In either case, you and I would be well-advised to decide ahead of time what our stance is toward the gospel of Jesus.

In February of 2015 the terrorist group known as ISIS released video of the beheading of 21 Egyptian Coptic Christian men. These men were martyred because of their faith in Jesus Christ. The men were dressed in orange jumpsuits and were led, single-file, by their murderers onto a beach prior to being killed. They were laid face-down on the sand and beheaded because they believed in Jesus.

Twenty-one Christians martyred because of their faith. They were not ashamed of the gospel of Jesus Christ. Their testimony will speak of their faith for decades to come.

What about you, friend? What about me? I hope I would be faithful to Jesus in the same situation. My prayer is that I would not turn away from giving my life for the gospel. I want to be bold and courageous in the face of persecution, trusting the Holy Spirit to lead and guide my words and actions.

Every day we have opportunities to share Jesus with those around us. Do you? Do I? He gave His life so that we could live eternally with Him in heaven. Each time we fail to share the gospel with others because of fear of what they will think or say, we are saying that we are ashamed of the gospel of Jesus.

We have what the world needs. We have Jesus, and it is our responsibility to share Him with the world…even if it means ridicule or death. Are you ashamed of the gospel of Jesus?

WHAT'S COOKING? How did God speak to you today?

DAY 2 – God Never Wastes a Trial

Not long ago my husband asked me to make a list of things that would define me. When I asked him to explain what he meant, he said, "Write down things you say or habits you have that are uniquely yours. For example, you often say that 'God never wastes a trial.'"

He was right. I do say that pretty often because it is true. I know it. I've lived it. I see it happen every single day in my own life. God takes our test and turns it into our TEST-imony if we will let Him. He uses the difficulties and heartaches that we have been through to encourage and bless others who are going through the same thing.

God took the eating disorder that I struggled with earlier in my life and now allows me to walk alongside others going through the same thing.

He instilled in me compassion toward those dealing with aging and sick parents by allowing me to walk with my parents through cancer and dementia.

God took family estrangement that nearly destroyed me and gave me opportunities to speak encouragement and hope into others who are experiencing brokenness in their family.

Over and over, God uses what we think will kill us to make us a stronger witness for Christ and a source of comfort and encouragement for others. Paul, the apostle, knew this firsthand. The Corinthian church was going through a spot of trouble and trial when Paul mentored them on this concept of "test into testimony." Let's see what Paul told them.

Please turn to **2 Corinthians 1:3-11**. Read this passage, then answer the following questions:

In verse 3, what is Paul's general mood? Circle the correct answer.

Anger at God over trials he endured

Praise to God

Questioning God about his trials

How does Paul describe God in verse 3?

_____

_____

_____

Verse 4 tells us that God comforts us in our troubles for a specific reason. Note that reason here.

_____

_____

_____

These are not just pretty words or platitudes from Paul. He speaks from experience. How did Paul describe the experiences that gave him this knowledge? These are detailed in verses 8 and 9.

_____

_____

Paul, the great apostle, the New Testament hero of our faith, had been so distressed and pressed and troubled that he was ready to give up and die. Does this picture of Paul surprise you? It shouldn't because Paul was just like you and me. He was not perfect. He had trials, trouble, and yes, even despair and depression. Yet, Paul knew that God was with him and would care for him.

Perhaps you are walking through a time of trial and despair. Paul and I are here to offer you some encouragement.

God is near. Even though you may not be able to feel Him, He is with you.

God is able to keep you in the midst of the trial. He has plans and purpose for what you are going through. Trust His heart, friend.

God will use what you are experiencing to strengthen you and encourage others.

In the middle of trouble and trial it is difficult to see the bigger picture. Circumstances are overwhelming. Your heart may be shattered in a million pieces. Tears flow daily, and sometimes hourly. It would be so easy to just give up. But don't! Trust that God is near. Trust that He will keep you. Trust that He will turn your test into your testimony. This is where the rubber of faith meets the road of trial.

I will leave you with a quote that is another of my signature quotes. It is by Charles Spurgeon and fits beautifully with our discussion for today.

God is too good to be unkind; He is too wise to be mistaken.
When you cannot trace His hand, you can always trust His heart.

WHAT'S COOKING? How did God speak to you today?

_____

_____

_____

_____

_____

_____

_____

DAY 3 – The Table of Jesus

How long have you been a follower of Jesus Christ? Perhaps you can number the time, in decades, since you asked Him to be your Lord and Savior? For some of you it has been just a few years, or months, or days. Whatever the length of time, you probably have experienced the observance of the Lord's Supper, or Communion.

I began observing the Lord's Supper in my teens with what I perceived to be the appropriate amount of respect. Although, there was that time in high school when my friend spilled grape juice all over her beautiful white eyelet dress, and our row of teenagers erupted in giggles. Ah, but that was not the norm for us. We knew better than to be disruptive or disrespectful in church. The Lord's Supper was a time when we were especially quiet and solemn.

I looked forward with eager anticipation to these observances. Whether it was because it was something different in the usual order of worship, or because I felt a teeny bit closer to Jesus when I held that tiny cup of juice and piece of bread, the quarterly observance held great appeal for me.

When I made my first pilgrimage to Israel in 2006, we celebrated the Lord's Supper in the Garden just outside the area of the empty tomb. We sat as a group, and our pastor passed out the elements. Each of us was given a tiny olive wood chalice from which we drank the juice. Just as we finished the ceremony, another group, somewhere in the garden, began singing in another language a song we knew well. As they sang in their language, we sang in English, "Because He Lives" by Bill and Gloria Gaither.

As long as I breathe earth's air, I'll never forget the indescribable holiness of that moment. I'm certain it was a breathtaking preview of what we will experience in heaven around the throne of God when every nation, tribe, and tongue worships the risen and reigning King of Kings, Jesus Christ.

About a year ago, I was studying 1 Corinthians 11 when I came across a passage that speaks about the Lord's Supper. I want you to read it. Please turn to **1 Corinthians 11:17-30** and prayerfully read the passage; then answer the following questions:

Paul tells us that it is possible to observe the Lord's Supper in an unworthy manner. Those who do this will be guilty of what?

_____

_____

_____

_____

Verse 28 tells us what we need to do in order to avoid coming to the Lord's Table in an unworthy manner. What is that?

_____

_____

_____

Failing to examine oneself prior to observing the Supper and coming to the table wrongly brings judgment, according to Paul. He, then, goes on in verse 30 to list some of the consequences of this sin. Please list them here.

_____

_____

_____

_____

A good question to ask ourselves at this point is, "How does this apply to me?" This was where my "aha" moment happened a few months ago. It is embarrassing to admit, but I had never taken this passage seriously.

Yes, I was quiet when I came to the table. I was reverent. I was solemn. What I had failed to do, however, was to examine my heart before coming to the table of the Lord. I had not been intentional about asking the Lord to show me any sin that I was harboring in my heart. I had not confessed sin and asked forgiveness in those moments prior to taking the elements of supper. It never occurred to me that I was taking the supper in an unworthy manner.

I would never think of pulling up a chair to the table in your home or mine without washing my hands and making sure I was clean and ready to eat. Why in the world had I failed to prepare myself for the Lord's Supper?

What about you? Are you intentional in your preparation for Communion? Do you search your heart in the moments and hours prior to partaking of the supper in order to assure that you come with clean hands and a clean heart?

I do not want to be guilty of approaching the table of our Lord in an inappropriate manner, and neither do you. Wash up, friend, and let's commune with our Lord in beauty and holiness.

WHAT'S COOKING? How did God speak to you today?

_____

_____

_____

_____

_____

DAY 4 - PRAY OFTEN, PRAY ALWAYS

Here we are in the final two days of our *Tasting Grace* Bible study. As we have studied passages of Scripture this week that offer important mentoring tips, I feel the need to hone down to the basics on these final days. If I were your mentor and we were sitting across a table, sipping cups of coffee and nibbling on chocolate cobbler, there are two things I would tell you that I consider to be non-negotiable for walking the walk of Christ. Today we will look at the first, and tomorrow the second. These are not in order of importance because both are crucial. I simply wrote them as the Holy Spirit gave me inspiration.

Please look up the following Scriptures and write them out in the space provided.

Mark 6:46

_____

_____

_____

Luke 18:1

_____

_____

_____

1 Thessalonians 5:17

_____

_____

_____

1 Thessalonians 5:25

_____

_____

_____

Jude 20

_____

_____

_____

What is the common theme of each of these verses?

_____

_____

_____

If you said that the common theme of our focal verses today is prayer, you are correct. Prayer is the lifeline of the Christ-follower. It is the way we communicate with God, and I fear it is the spiritual discipline that is most lacking in the lives of the majority of believers…myself included.

My husband and I were huge fans of the television drama *24*. In the show, Keifer Sutherland played Jack Bauer, an agent employed by the fictitious Counter Terrorism Unit, or CTU. Bauer did not always follow the rules, especially when he saw a better way to take down the bad guys. On occasion, Jack would "go dark," and defy the orders of his superiors in order to accomplish the mission on which he was sent. In going dark, Bauer cut all communication with his CTU bosses and operated solely on his own.

While going dark always seemed to work out for Jack, it is never a good plan for a Christian. Any really good relationship requires two-way communication. The relationship between a husband and wife requires that both people talk and listen. The same is true between an employer and an employee, a parent and a child, a coach and a player, and any other situations where two or people must live and work in harmony.

In our relationship with Jesus, there must be good communication through prayer. We must present our prayers to God with our hearts humble, clean, and prepared to hear from Him. As we pray from a submitted, willing heart, Jesus intercedes for us before the throne in heaven. Then, the Holy Spirit speaks to us, guiding and directing us, according to the will of God. He may speak in many different ways: directly to our heart, through Scripture, through the words of another person, through a song or poem, through nature, or in any of a thousand different ways.

Our prayers do not have to contain certain words or be spoken for a set period of time. Neither do we have to have a specific place that we pray, although having a location set aside for a quiet time is a wonderful plan. We can pray at any time and in any place.

What God wants from us as we pray is a sincere heart that longs to communicate with Him. Sometimes our prayers contain beautiful words, while at other times our prayers are groans from deep within a hurting heart. God hears and answers both. I talk with the Lord on and off throughout the day. My prayers are not stiff, formal words but rather an on-going conversation with my best friend.

You and I must be diligent about our prayer life. Pray when you sit and when you stand. Pray when you work and when you rest. Pray when you are happy and when you are sad. Pray when you feel like it, and pray when you do not. Pray continually, friend. It is your lifeline to Jesus.

WHAT'S COOKING? How did God speak to you today?

_____

_____

_____

_____

_____

DAY 5 – Read the Instructions

When it comes to assembling something or learning how to use a new gadget, two types of people can be found at my house. One gives the instructions a cursory glance and plows in, attempting to figure the thing out on her own. The other sits down with the instructions, reads them well, makes sure he has all the appropriate parts and pieces, and then begins assembly or use. Since only one "he" and one "she" live at my house, it is not hard to discern which descriptor belongs to which person.

Greg is methodical and precise, while I just jump in and try to make it work. Often, he comes to my rescue when I reach a certain frustration point because of my lack of willingness to completely read and understand the instructions BEFORE beginning the task.

When something comes with instructions, we are wise to read them.

LIFE comes with instructions. God made sure of it. He gave us the Holy Scriptures to teach and guide us. He gave us the Holy Spirit to serve as our counselor and teacher. Unfortunately, all too often we fail to read the instruction manual before making a decision. Let's see what God has to say about this issue.

Read the following Scriptures from **Psalm 119** and match them to the truth they convey concerning God's Word.

Verse 11	It lights our path.
Verse 28	It keeps us from sin.
Verse 66	It is righteous and trustworthy.
Verse 89	It provides strength for the weary soul.
Verse 105	It is eternal.
Verse 138	It gives knowledge and good judgment.

The entire 119th chapter of the Book of Psalms extols the benefits of Scripture. It is like an advertisement for the Word of God. You and I are wise to read Psalm 119 in order to be reminded of the ways that Scripture impacts our lives. We are wiser still to live according to the whole counsel of God's Word.

Turn to **Proverbs 14:12**. Read this verse and then write it in the space below.

_____
_____
_____
_____

God has told us the right way to live; He has given us perfect instructions for life in the Bible. All too often we either fail to read the instruction manual, or we only read the parts of it that fit with what we want to do or be.

In Hebrews 4:12 we read that Scripture is living and active and able to speak into any situations in our lives. God gave Scripture for our good, not to cramp our style. When God gives us permission in Scripture to do a certain thing, we can be sure that thing is for our good. Likewise, when God forbids something, we can be equally certain that no good will come of pursuing it. God has a bigger perspective than we have. Consequently, when He says "no" to something it is because He knows the consequences of that action. God's "no" is for our good, and we should view it as a blessing from our loving Father.

I heard a man tell a story recently about a time in his youth when he wanted to participate in something that was destined to be trouble. It was an activity that the Bible said should not be part of the life of a follower of Jesus Christ. The young fella decided that he would just do it anyway and told his mother what he had decided.

With wisdom given to her from God, she looked at him and said, "Who do you think you are to decide that what God has called bad is really good? Just who do you think you are?"

This man said that those words from his mother stopped him dead in his tracks.

Friend, every decision you and I make should line up with Scripture. When we stubbornly insist on having our way and doing things that God cannot bless, we can be certain there will be severe consequences.

So, as we close our journey together today, I want to ask you a few questions. As your mentor on this journey, my heart's desire is to point you in the direction of Jesus.

- Do you know Jesus as your Lord and Savior?
- Does Jesus have all of your heart?
- Do you make prayer a priority each day?
- Are your life decisions and actions consistent with Scripture?

If you could not answer "yes" to each of these questions, please spend some time talking to Jesus, allowing the Holy Spirit to minister to your heart. Jesus loves you so. He wants a close, intimate relationship with you, but you must be willing to allow Him to mentor you through prayer and Scripture.

Jan and I are honored to have taken this *Tasting Grace* journey with you. It is our hope that you have drawn closer to Jesus and developed a heart for mentoring and cooking.

WHAT'S COOKING? How did God speak to you today?

_____

_____

_____

_____

Notes:

Leah's Homemade Biscuits

Your homemade biscuits will make you the most popular person in town! There are few things more pleasing than a hot, fresh, homemade biscuit slathered in butter and jam or honey. Many people think biscuits are difficult to make, but that simply is not true. Here is my recipe for biscuits that will win rave reviews every time you make them.

2 cups self-rising flour, sifted

¼ cup lard

⅔ to ¾ cup whole buttermilk (not fat free or low fat)

Baking spray

Preheat oven to 500° F.

Directions:
Sift 2 cups self-rising flour into a large bowl. Add in lard. Using your fingers, work the lard into the flour so that you end up with the lard evenly distributed throughout the flour. The lard should be in pieces less than the size of a pea. Add buttermilk to the lard and flour, mixing it in with your hands. The dough should pull away from the sides of the bowl and make a large lump. Make sure the ingredients are incorporated well, but don't over knead the dough. Sift approximately ⅛ cup of extra flour onto a clean, smooth surface. Turn the dough out onto the floured surface. Keep your hands floured so the dough does not stick to them. Pick up the dough, leaving as much of the flour on the surface as possible.

Knead the dough three to four times. Return the dough to the floured surface and flatten the dough until it is approximately 1 inch thick. Using a drinking glass or biscuit cutter, cut out the biscuits and place them on a greased pan. My preference is an iron skillet, but a cookie sheet or other oven-safe pan will work. When you have cut two to three biscuits and placed them on the pan, pick up the remaining dough (leaving as much of the flour on the surface as possible) and reshape it into a circle.

Repeat the rolling out, cutting, and shaping process until you have used all the dough. Place all biscuits on the pan—very close or almost touching each other. The closer they are to each other, the more they will rise. Place in the oven and cook for 8–10 minutes or until golden brown. Melt ¼ stick of butter in the microwave. When the biscuits are done, immediately brush them with the melted butter. Enjoy!

Cheesy Apple Cobbler

2 cans fried apples

1 stick margarine or butter

4-6 oz. Velveeta Cheese

1 cup sugar

¾ cup self-rising flour

Cinnamon, sprinkled to taste

Preheat oven to 350° F.

Directions:

Drain apples. Mix together all other ingredients and melt in microwave. Add apples and mix well. (At this point, you can refrigerate until ready to cook and serve if desired). Spread in 9" x 9" baking dish coated with baking spray. Bake at 350° for 20–30 minutes, or until browned slightly. Serve warm, alone or with vanilla ice cream. This dish is like an apple cobbler with cheese. Pure comfort food!

Notes:

Tomato Pie

1 refrigerated piecrust (store-bought ☺)

3 large, ripe tomatoes

1 large Vidalia (or sweet) onion

¾ cup mayonnaise

1 ½ cups grated medium to sharp cheddar cheese

Salt, pepper, and fresh basil to garnish

Preheat oven to 350° F.

Directions:

Roll out piecrust and place in a deep-dish pie plate—prebake crust for 5-6 minutes. Peel tomatoes and cut into thick slices, drain on paper towels. Slice onion into thin slices. Cover bottom of crust with a layer of sliced tomatoes. Place thin onion slices over layer of tomatoes. Sprinkle with salt and pepper—be generous with the pepper!

Spread half of mayonnaise over onions. Repeat tomatoes, onions, and mayo for a second layer. Salt and pepper again. Cover top of pie with grated cheese. Bake 15-20 minutes until crust is light brown and cheese is melted. Remove and cool. Do not cut until pie is room temperature.

Peach Cobbler

May use other fruit such as blueberries, blackberries or strawberries.

8″ x 8″ casserole dish

7 medium size fresh peaches (or 2 ½ cups of berries)

3 cups water

1 ½ cups sugar

1 stick butter

1 cup self-rising flour

1 cup milk (not skim)

1 cup sugar

Preheat oven to 350° F.

Directions:

Peel and slice peaches. Make a simple syrup by bringing 3 cups of water and 1 ½ cups of sugar to boil. Add fruit and simmer 10-12 minutes. Melt the butter in an 8″× 8″ casserole dish.

Mix one cup self-rising flour, one cup sugar, and one cup 2% or whole milk with wire whisk until all lumps are gone and it is smooth! Pour this batter over the melted butter and DO NOT STIR! Gently ladle in the peaches and simple syrup over the batter. DO NOT STIR!

Place into preheated oven. Bake 35-45 minutes (you know your oven) until cobbler is golden brown and crust has risen to the top! Serve the cobbler while warm with a scoop of vanilla ice cream on top.

Chocolate Cobbler

6 tablespoons butter

1 cup self-rising flour

¾ cup white sugar

1 ½ tablespoons unsweetened cocoa powder

½ cup milk

1 teaspoon vanilla extract

1 cup white sugar

¼ cup unsweetened cocoa powder

1 ½ cups boiling water

Preheat oven to 350° F. Melt butter in an 8" x 8" baking dish in the oven while it preheats.

Directions:
In a medium bowl, stir together flour, ¾ cup sugar, and 1 ½ tablespoon cocoa. Stir in milk and vanilla until smooth. Spoon this batter over the melted butter in the baking dish. Stir together the remaining 1-cup of sugar and ¼ cup cocoa powder. Sprinkle over batter. Pour boiling water over the top of the mixture. Bake until set for 30-35 minutes in the preheated oven. The crust will rise to the top. The cobbler is wonderful as is, or it can be served while still warm with a scoop of vanilla ice cream on top.

Notes:

_____

_____

_____

_____

_____

_____

_____

_____

_____

_____

Grandma Eula's Homemade Chicken and Dumplings

1 chicken, stewed and deboned with some of the skin remaining

1 quart or larger chicken broth

2 cups self-rising flour

¼ cup lard or Crisco® shortening

Buttermilk—approximately ⅔ - ¾ cup

One stick REAL butter

1 TBSP salt

1 TBSP black pepper

Directions:

To be honest, these amounts are negotiable. Grandma Colwell did not give amounts in her recipe, and so I just guess about everything. These are really easy, I promise.

Stew the chicken in large pot of water and/or chicken broth for 1 hour. Cool until you can handle comfortably. Pull the meat off the bone, placing half of it back in the pot with the liquid, and discard bone. Keep the other half to add back in after your dumplings are cooked.

Make very firm dumpling dough, using biscuit recipe from Week 1. You will use a bit less buttermilk for dumplings than you do for biscuits. Allow the dough to rise in a warm place for up to 2 hours. Bring chicken and broth to boil. Add in butter, salt and pepper. Knead dough a couple of times on a floured surface and roll out very, very thin, using a rolling pin. I usually roll out my dough in two batches.

With a blunt knife, cut strips of dumplings. I cut mine about 1 inch wide and 2-3 inches long. Do whatever suits you. Drop dumplings into boiling pot a few at a time, allowing some of the flour from the surface where you rolled out the dough to go into the pot along with the dough. The flour helps the liquid thicken.

Once the first batch of dough is in the pot, turn the heat down to low, cover the pot, and allow it to cook while you roll out and cut the second batch of dough.

Turn the heat back to high and drop the second batch of dumplings in the pot. Make sure you stir gently between batches so the chicken doesn't stick to the bottom of the pan. After the second batch of dumplings is in the pot, turn the heat to medium, replace the lid on the pot, and allow it to cook for about 10 minutes. Turn off the heat and let the dumplings sit until you are ready to eat.

I usually make my chicken and dumplings up to two hours before we want to eat them. This allows the liquid to thicken up a bit. I don't rewarm them before serving, but you could. Enjoy and know my Grandma Colwell is smiling on you!

Gran Jan's Cornbread Recipe

1 ½ cups White Lily self-rising buttermilk cornmeal

½ cup of White Lily self-rising flour

1 egg

1 ½ cups buttermilk

¼ cup oil

Crisco or Lard (to grease skillet)

Directions:
Preheat oven to 450°. Mix oil and egg, add buttermilk, and then cornmeal and flour. Mix the wet and dry ingredients well. Generously grease a cast-iron skillet with Crisco. Sprinkle dry cornmeal over the Crisco in the pan. Pour the cornbread mixture in the skillet. Bake 20-25 minutes until nicely browned.

Notes:

_____
_____
_____
_____
_____
_____
_____
_____
_____
_____
_____
_____
_____
_____
_____
_____
_____
_____
_____

Jan's Cornbread Dressing

*Cornbread dressing is a staple of Southern Thanksgiving tables. Here is a basic recipe with variations included at the end. Experiment and discover what your family loves and make it your own! Basically, **Southern Cornbread Dressing** is comprised of good broth and a mixture of ⅔ cornbread and ⅓ white bread (or biscuits or even saltine crackers). You can buy canned broth, but if you'll take time and make your own broth it is the best! If possible, put the dressing together the day before you intend to bake it in order to allow time for the flavors to meld.* **MAKES 9" x 13" PAN**

1 pan of cornbread, crumbled – about 7-8 cups (see cornbread recipe)

White bread or biscuits (allowed to dry out), crumbled – about 3 cups (OR ½ sleeve crushed saltines).

Salt and black pepper to taste

2 tsp. poultry seasoning (optional)

3 eggs, beaten

1 stick butter (softened) to sauté celery and onion

1 ½ cups celery and 1 large onion [or to taste] (chop fine and sauté in butter until soft)

1 can herbed cream of chicken soup (or plain cream of chicken soup)

Chicken stock/broth (BOIL 2 ½ quarts of water, salt, pepper, 3-4 chicken thighs or if you are roasting a turkey, you may use the turkey neck, ½ stick of butter, 2 chopped onions, 2-3 stalks of celery-include leaves.) [You won't use ALL the broth, but you can freeze to use later as soup base.]

Preheat oven to 400° F.

Directions:
Grease 9" x 13" pan. In a large bowl, crumble cornbread and dried white bread slices (or saltines, biscuits). Melt butter in a large skillet over medium heat and add chopped celery and onion. Cook until transparent, about 5 to 10 minutes. Pour celery and onion mixture over the cornbread mixture.

Strain your chicken stock and pour hot broth over cornbread and mix well. You want the dressing to be the consistency of oatmeal, not too soupy, not too thick. **TASTE NOW BEFORE ADDING EGGS!** Add salt & pepper to taste (and sage or poultry seasoning if you use them—LESS IS MORE!)

Add 3 beaten eggs and mix well. Pour into greased casserole pan and bake at 400°- 425° until browned on top, about 30-45 minutes.

Continued on next page.

VARIATIONS:
- A small jar of chopped pimentos for color, be sure to drain first
- Bag of Pepperidge Farm Herb Stuffing for more herbed flavor
- Poultry Seasoning (to taste)
- Sage seasoning (to taste)
- Canned chicken broth instead of homemade
- Leave out celery
- Add cooked chopped turkey or chicken to the dressing prior to baking

Layered Mexican Chicken Salad

1 cup ranch dressing

2 tsp taco seasoning mix

4 cups Romaine or other lettuce, torn or shredded

1 can black beans, or other bean of choice, drained

1 can whole kernel corn, drained

1 small onion, chopped

1 bell pepper, color of choice, chopped

Meat of 1 deli rotisserie chicken, chopped

1 - 2 cups Hint-o-Lime tortilla chips or other lime-flavored tortilla chips, crushed coarsely

1 cup shredded Mexican-style cheese

¾ cup grape or cherry tomatoes

Directions:
Mix dressing with taco seasoning. Set aside. Layer lettuce through cheese in order in a large dish. Drizzle with dressing. Place tomatoes on top as garnish.

LEADERS' GUIDE/EVENT PLANNER

How To Use *Tasting Grace*...
A Mentoring-in-the Kitchen Bible Study Experience

Jan and I are excited that you have been drawn to a ministry that we have seen bless so many women, including the two of us. In truth, it has blessed many men too. We have had husbands ask when we will be doing our next cooking class because their wives came home from one and made them a delicious meal! It could easily work the other way around, too—men come to a *Tasting Grace* event, then go home to prepare their wives a yummy meal! We believe that every person, woman or man, can be a mentor in the kitchen and in life.

You may be curious about how *Tasting Grace* works. It is really very easy but does take a bit of planning and preparation. Allow me to explain.

The book is divided into three sections:
The Word – Bible Study for four weeks (Pages 7-54)
Tasting Grace Recipes (Pages 55-62)
Leaders' Guide/Event Planner (Pages 63-88)

Within each section of the Leaders' Guide are two parts:
Chapter 1 – The Idea
    Our Ideas – Basic information about our *Tasting Grace events*
    Your Tools – 2 Devotionals and 2 Recipes

Chapter 2 – The Invitation
    Our Invitations – How we invited ladies to our events
    Your Tools – 2 Devotionals and 2 Recipes

Chapter 3 – The Preparation
    Our Preparation – How we prepare for our events; i.e. set-up, grocery shopping, and so forth.
    Your Tools – 2 Devotionals and 2 Recipes

Chapter 4 – The Event
    Our Events – Sharing a bit about our *Tasting Grace* events
    Your Tools – 2 Devotionals and 2 Recipes

There are two possible ways for you to use this book: in a group setting or for your personal spiritual enrichment as an individual. We hope you will use it to take a small group of ladies, or men, through a journey of Bible study and learning to cook.

Allow us to offer you a few suggestions for how a group might use the book.

The size of your group will depend on the size of the kitchen facilities you have available. Once you have determined the number of participants in your group, purchase a book for each person.

Pray diligently for the group, asking Jesus to lead and direct as you mentor the group in the Scriptures and in the kitchen.

When you meet the first week (Introduction Week), you might want to have beverages and snacks for the group, but it is not necessary. If you have group members who do not know each other, it is always a good idea to have nametags for each person.

Once everyone arrives, pass out the books and explain that there are five days of homework in each week of the study. Encourage the members to complete their homework, which will take about 10-15 minutes each day. Remind them that even if they are not able to complete all the homework, coming to class each week for the Bible study discussion and cooking class will benefit them.

To set the stage for their time in the Scriptures, you will want to choose one of the devotionals from the workbook and present it to the group in this first meeting, or you may use your own devotional material. Either way, emphasize to the group that spending time in the Scriptures is a crucial part of this study. You may choose to do a devotional from the book each subsequent week, or allow the homework discussion to serve as time in the Scripture, depending on the amount of time allotted for each class.

Choose one of the Week One recipes or a recipe of your own to prepare at the **next meeting,** and let the group know which one it is. You might want to ask group members to contribute different ingredients for the recipe. Let them know that each week's cooking class will be hands-on for them. They will be doing the cooking, while you lead them through the steps and assist as needed.

TASTING GRACE TIPS

Cover your event in prayer. Ask the Lord to guide you regarding date, time, location, menu, and how to effectively invite women to your Tasting Grace event.

If you are making biscuits at your event, allow each lady to make her own batch. Then have paper bags or foil available so she can take the rest of her biscuits home to her family.

If you are making multiple dishes, you may want to allow your ladies to work together to prepare them. Please turn to page 76 and read the paragraphs under Our Preparation

Make sure you schedule time for a short devotional (10 minutes or less) and time at the end for the ladies to taste their creations.

You may want to charge a fee for the event if you are hosting it in your home. If your church is sponsoring the event, they may cover the fee for the ladies. This will help cover the cost of ingredients and other necessary supplies.

Weeks One - Three

Welcome group members into the class. Depending on the recipe you are preparing this week and how much cooking/baking time is needed, you might want to begin with the cooking class and finish up with the Bible study discussion. If actual cooking time is minimal, you may discuss the homework first, and then move into the kitchen to cook. Do whatever works for your group, but please make sure you allow sufficient time to discuss the Bible study homework.

The Bible study discussion can be either a general overview of the homework or a page-by-page discussion. We encourage you to offer ample opportunity for group members to ask questions and interact in the discussion of Scripture. Allow the living and active Word of God to teach your group each week.

At the end of your time together each week, while your group tastes their creations, remind the group about the next 5 days of Bible study homework. Also let them know which recipe will be prepared the next week and ask for volunteers who will bring ingredients for the dish.

Week Four

This week will be the grand finale! You might want to schedule extra time and prepare more than one dish. If you choose to prepare multiple dishes, divide your group into teams, with each team being responsible for the preparation of one dish.

Even if you schedule extra cooking time, please do not skip over the Bible study discussion. Our experience is that the homework discussion is where most of the learning takes place.

Once the group has finished all four weeks of the study, take a deep breath and give yourself a pat on the back. You have mentored your group in the Scriptures, as well as equipped and empowered them to feel comfortable in the kitchen, making wonderful dishes for their family. You have planted proverbial trees under which you may never sit, but which will yield abundant fruit in the lives and hearts of your group members. Congratulations and well done!

WEEK ONE - THE IDEA

Welcome to Week One of *Tasting Grace*! This week our focus is on the idea of mentoring. The idea of a mentoring-in-the-kitchen ministry started with Jan, so she will share a bit about how she began her ministry.

Without a doubt, homemade biscuits are the most popular menu item at *Tasting Grace*. Perhaps that is because Jan and I live in the South. Please do not be intimated by homemade biscuits. There is an art to them and practice makes perfect!

Finally, you will come to the Bible study portion that focuses on mentoring in the Scriptures. We hope you will fully engage your heart in the study of God's Word. When you do, we believe you will fall in love with it. As you pass on cooking skills to other women, you can also pass on your love of God's Word.

Now, it is time to get started. Grab your apron, friend, and let's begin our mentoring-in-the-kitchen journey!

 **OUR IDEAS**

Hello! I'm Jan Morton and I've been serving in Women's Ministry for over 17 years. As a women's ministry leader today, I recognize how ministry to women is changing. I believe most women desire authenticity, purpose, and real connections.

A few years ago, God began to stir my heart toward a new ministry to women. Even with all the ways for young women to connect through social media, nothing ever replaces a face-to-face conversation that provides the close relationships for which they long. In this fast food, fast-paced world in which we live, there is something truly special about gathering around a good meal at the table.

That's where **TASTE & SEE** (Jan's name for her *Tasting Grace*-type event) was born! The name of our event is taken from Psalm 34:8 - *Taste and see that the LORD is good. Oh, the joys of those who take refuge in him!* My sweet friend, Jan Hamil, and I work together in this outreach, where we encourage women of all ages to connect and share together while learning cooking (and life) skills.

I've heard many women say over the years that the quilting bees and sewing circles of long ago were vital places for women to share and bond, and we girls know…it wasn't all about the quilting! Women need women like never before in our social- media-driven society. I'm thankful to have the blessing of sharing my life's experiences and love for cooking with these precious young women.

When I was a young pastor's wife, I had the same blessings from older women in my life, but we didn't know it was *mentoring*. I still thank God for Mrs. Tricia, who shared her pot roast recipe with me when she had our young family over for Sunday lunch. In fact, I wrote her a long letter not long ago thanking her for her influence in my life. We were just doing life, and mentoring happened along the way. Nothing forced or organized; it was just the pure joy of coming alongside another woman to be an encourager.

You can't get that from a computer screen, texting, Snapchat, Facebook, or Instagram. I certainly don't want to take away from modern technology, because I sure do love my convection oven, Kitchen Aid stand mixer, dishwasher, and air conditioning! We wouldn't have had nearly as much fun at **TASTE & SEE** if we'd had to chop wood to load into the stove before making our biscuits!

 YOUR TOOLS - DEVOTIONALS

#1 - Proverbs 2:6

Read aloud Proverbs 2:6.

We need wisdom today. There are a multitude of words that are spoken and written through radio, television, the Internet, and conversation, but how much of it is true wisdom?

As we consider this word "wisdom," we find that the original Hebrew word used by the writer of Proverbs suggests skillfulness, insight, knowledge, and judgment.

Offer an example from your own life where you gained wisdom, insight, and skill from a life circumstance; i.e. learning to cook, learning a craft or trade, and so forth.

Read Proverbs 2:1-6 to the group, emphasizing the action words or verbs in the passage. (Getting wisdom is not a passive process. We cannot simply sit down and expect to rise in ten minutes a much wiser person. We must actively pursue wisdom as detailed in these verses.)

Ask the group to consider verse 6 once again. (If true wisdom is given by God and comes from His mouth, then where should we go to find that wisdom?) Hopefully your group will answer that we find true wisdom through studying Scripture and communicating with God through prayer.

Remind the group that if they want true wisdom they should begin reading and studying the Bible every day. Encourage them to spend time in the book of Proverbs.

#2 – Proverbs 27:17

Read Proverbs 27:17 aloud.

Iron is a hard metal. When it stands in need of sharpening, only certain materials will do the job. You cannot sharpen iron with cotton, rubber, or wood. Iron must be sharpened with an instrument harder and more durable than it.

So it is with humans. Our hearts can become dull to the things of God, which creates a crisis of need in our lives. Often God will send someone alongside us who is more mature in his or her walk with the Lord. That person will be used by Jesus to sharpen us and encourage us in our own walk with Him. It may be a friend, pastor, mentor, boss, or a complete stranger. God can use anyone or anything to sharpen us—often He allows trials. He may use the lack of finances, marriage troubles, major illnesses, wayward children, or job difficulties to sharpen us.

Each time God chooses the perfect instrument for our situation. Oh, it may not feel perfect; in fact, it may feel very uncomfortable, even painful. It may cause hurt and rips in the fabric of our hearts. But God's goal is sharpening us so that we look more and more like Jesus. We are wise to bend our knee to the instrument that God sends for our sharpening.

Ask the group how they are being sharpened in this season.

Notes:

_____
_____
_____
_____
_____
_____
_____
_____
_____
_____
_____
_____
_____
_____
_____
_____
_____
_____

RECIPES FOR WEEK 1

#1 - Leah's Homemade Biscuits

Your homemade biscuits will make you the most popular person in town! There are few things more pleasing than a hot, fresh, homemade biscuit slathered in butter and jam or honey. Many people think biscuits are difficult to make, but that simply is not true. Here is my recipe for biscuits that will win rave reviews every time you make them.

2 cups self-rising flour, sifted

¼ cup lard

⅔ to ¾ cup whole buttermilk (not fat free or low fat)

Baking spray

Preheat oven to 500° F.

Directions:
Sift 2 cups self-rising flour into a large bowl. Add in lard. Using your fingers, work the lard into the flour so that you end up with the lard evenly distributed throughout the flour. The lard should be in pieces less than the size of a pea. Add buttermilk to the lard and flour, mixing it in with your hands. The dough should pull away from the sides of the bowl and make a large lump. Make sure the ingredients are incorporated well, but don't over knead the dough. Sift approximately ⅛ cup of extra flour onto a clean, smooth surface. Turn the dough out onto the floured surface. Keep your hands floured so the dough does not stick to them. Pick up the dough, leaving as much of the flour on the surface as possible.

Knead the dough three to four times. Return the dough to the floured surface and flatten the dough until it is approximately 1 inch thick. Using a drinking glass or biscuit cutter, cut out the biscuits and place them on a greased pan. My preference is an iron skillet, but a cookie sheet or other oven-safe pan will work. When you have cut two to three biscuits and placed them on the pan, pick up the remaining dough (leaving as much of the flour on the surface as possible) and reshape it into a circle.

Repeat the rolling out, cutting, and shaping process until you have used all the dough. Place all biscuits on the pan—very close or almost touching each other. The closer they are to each other, the more they will rise. Place in the oven and cook for 8–10 minutes or until golden brown. Melt ¼ stick of butter in the microwave. When the biscuits are done, immediately brush them with the melted butter. Enjoy!

#2 - Cheesy Apple Cobbler

2 cans fried apples

1 stick margarine or butter

4-6 oz. Velveeta Cheese

1 cup sugar

¾ cup self-rising flour

Cinnamon, sprinkled to taste

Preheat oven to 350° F.

Directions:
Drain apples. Mix together all other ingredients and melt in microwave. Add apples and mix well. (At this point, you can refrigerate until ready to cook and serve if desired). Spread in 9" x 9" baking dish coated with baking spray. Bake at 350° for 20–30 minutes, or until browned slightly. Serve warm, alone or with vanilla ice cream. This dish is like an apple cobbler with cheese. Pure comfort food!

Notes:

WEEK TWO – The Invitation

Come. Be part of. Partake. Enjoy. Join us.

An invitation may be printed on parchment using beautiful calligraphy, or it might be a simple text message that shows up on your mobile device. Either way, an invitation creates anticipation and excitement. There is a sense of belonging that comes with an invitation because someone desires your presence at an event.

This week you will learn a bit about the way Jan and I invite ladies to our *Tasting Grace* events. You will find two more recipes and two devotionals this week as well.

We want to give you a disclaimer right now: this book is rich in cobbler recipes. Jan and I are southern women and in the South, cobblers reign supreme. Never fear, though, if you are not a cobbler person, you will find other recipes to entice your taste buds.

Please feel free to use the space in the back of the book to think through your invitation for your event. You might want to create your guest list here, or sketch out what you want your invitation to look like.

 OUR INVITATION

Hello! This is Leah. Jan and I live on opposite ends of the state of Georgia, but thanks to the Internet and social media, we can communicate any time we want. Early in 2015 when I saw Jan's blog post detailing her inaugural *Taste & See* event, my heart went pitter-patter. From the first paragraph, I was hooked. Immediately, I began to ask the Lord if it might be His will that I host some ladies for a similar event. When God gave the green light, I got to work planning and preparing.

I used social media exclusively to invite ladies to my events. I tossed out a very casual invitation on my personal Facebook page for the first *Tasting Grace* event and received immediate responses from several ladies. Facebook's Messenger application was a great tool for me to use to stay in touch with my ladies, giving them updates on the event and directions to the venue.

I also created a private Facebook page to which I added each lady who attended a *Tasting Grace* event. That private page is where I post recipes, devotional thoughts, and sneak previews of upcoming events for them. Previous *Tasting Grace* attendees are offered early registration through the private group page for upcoming events.

Jan holds her events in the kitchen at her church. She uses announcements in the church bulletin, as well as verbal announcements from the platform to create an invitation for ladies to join her.

You can make your invitation as unique as you want it to be. Jan and I are both apron-wearing women, and we encourage our attendees to bring their own apron to the event. It is always fun to see the unique aprons that show up at *Tasting Grace*.

YOUR TOOLS - DEVOTIONALS

#1 – Ecclesiastes 3:1

Read the verse to your group.

The Word says: For everything [it does say *everything*], there is a season and a time for every matter/purpose/activity under heaven (Leah's version).

Everything defined as "the entirety of; a great deal, especially of something very important." EVERYTHING!

All of life relates to seasons—from the beauty found in the four seasons of a calendar year to the seasons of our lives. *Talk about the season you are in currently in your life.*

What is your season of womanhood right now?

Are you in SPRING – a young woman in school or just beginning a career? Perhaps you are newly married? How about SUMMER – in the "zone" raising children or building a career or marriage? Maybe you're in AUTUMN – children grown, and you may be looking toward retirement? Or perhaps you find yourself in WINTER – your senior years as a woman, perhaps a widow, reflecting on past seasons and all God has brought you through.

WHEREVER YOU ARE, BE ALL THERE. In the busyness of life, it is easy to lose focus. Don't be longing for another season and miss what's going on around you now. This deception is one of the biggest lies of the enemy of our souls…the distraction and discontentment with where we are today. Embrace your season!

Here is an acrostic for the word SEASON –
> **S**avor
> **E**very
> **A**vailable
> **S**ent
> **O**pportunity
> **N**ow

Some seasons are more enjoyable than others, to be sure! Just as changes in seasons bring mosquitoes in summer or storms in winter, there are extremes in our lives. Some of you empty nesters may suddenly find yourselves caring for both your grandchildren and aging parents. Some young women may be longing for marriage. Stay-at-home moms, or single moms, may have to go into the workforce for a season to pay the bills. If our entire lives were one continuous season, we wouldn't have the changes we desperately need to help us grow. You may love to garden, but if every day were spring or summer, there would be no autumn to harvest or winter to dream and plan.

Here are some things that the seasons of life may teach.

- Our constant, never-changing, faithful Lord Jesus is with us in every SEASON, in everything.
- Sometimes seasons overlap—several might descend on you at once.
- Sometimes joy and sorrow meet in a season.
- You may think springtime has come, but unseasonal cold snaps may occur and you better be ready. Life can throw trials at us in the blink of an eye. Memorizing God's Word is a lifeline in those times.
- Ask God to give you a strong focus in your season today and receive it as the gift it is, embracing the wonder. God will provide your daily bread.

"Which is the happiest season of life?" an older woman was asked. She replied, "When spring comes, and the flower buds are breaking through I think, 'How beautiful is spring.' And then when summer comes and covers the trees with heavy foliage and singing birds are among the branches, I think, 'How beautiful is summer.' When autumn arrives with golden fruit, and the leaves bear the gorgeous colors, I think, 'How beautiful is autumn.' And then comes winter, and there is neither foliage nor fruit, and I look up through the leafless branches as I never could until now, and see the stars shining in God's home. (Anonymous).

Embrace whatever season you are in now. RIGHT NOW. Don't long for another season. I know the days may be long, but the years seem so short. So wherever you are, be all there. Because of Jesus, one day we will be "SEASONED TO PERFECTION" and live with Christ for eternity.

#2 – 1 Kings 17:8-16

Can we ever get "enough?" How many times have you been enjoying a meal and the hostess asks, "Did you get enough to eat?"

Do you have enough? In this fast-paced, self-indulgent society in which we live, do you think people are ever truly satisfied? Have you ever attended the birthday party of a young child? It is all about the birthday girl or boy, and all the presents are his or hers to enjoy. Often there will be some others at the party who are not so happy. Why? Because they didn't have enough… mostly they lacked enough attention.

Did you know that comparison is the thief of joy? If we think someone has *more* or *better* of anything than we have, we can easily become discontented.

Remember these three words: *We get enough.* We really do, BECAUSE JESUS IS ENOUGH! *Don't ever forget that!*

Sometimes when we are too busy comparing ourselves with others, we can forget our own blessings, our own lives that are full and "enough!" Your life, your offering of ministry to Jesus, mothering your children, working at your job, and making a home for your family—these are enough!

Read **1 Kings 17:8-16** to your group.

Elijah assured this widow that there would be enough. She had nothing, but we see in verse 15 "*so she did as Elijah said.*" She was obedient and she believed the prophet. She placed confidence in the authority of the man of God. And what do we find in verse 16? There was **always enough** flour and olive oil left in the containers. She gave out of her lack and God provided. HE IS ENOUGH! He is always enough. No matter what you are going through, you can be sure of the certainty of abundance in Christ.

> We have enough…because *Jesus is enough.*
> We have enough…because *God is enough.*
> We have enough…because *the fullness of His Spirit is enough.*
> We have enough…because *His grace is sufficient—it is enough.*
> We have enough…because *the greatest of these is LOVE—His Love* is always ENOUGH!

RECIPES FOR WEEK 2

#1 - Tomato Pie

1 refrigerated piecrust (store-bought ☺)

3 large, ripe tomatoes

1 large Vidalia (or sweet) onion

¾ cup mayonnaise

1 ½ cups grated medium to sharp cheddar cheese

Salt, pepper, and fresh basil to garnish

Preheat oven to 350° F.

Directions:
Roll out piecrust and place in a deep-dish pie plate—prebake crust for 5-6 minutes. Peel tomatoes and cut into thick slices, drain on paper towels. Slice onion into thin slices. Cover bottom of crust with a layer of sliced tomatoes. Place thin onion slices over layer of tomatoes. Sprinkle with salt and pepper—be generous with the pepper!

Spread half of mayonnaise over onions. Repeat tomatoes, onions, and mayo for a second layer. Salt and pepper again. Cover top of pie with grated cheese. Bake 15-20 minutes until crust is light brown and cheese is melted. Remove and cool. Do not cut until pie is room temperature.

#2 - Peach Cobbler

May use other fruit such as blueberries, blackberries or strawberries.

8" x 8" casserole dish

7 medium size fresh peaches (or 2 ½ cups of berries)

3 cups water

1 ½ cups sugar

1 stick butter

1 cup self-rising flour

1 cup milk (not skim)

1 cup sugar

Preheat oven to 350° F.

Directions:

Peel and slice peaches. Make a simple syrup by bringing 3 cups of water and 1 ½ cups of sugar to boil. Add fruit and simmer 10-12 minutes. Melt the butter in an 8" x 8" casserole dish.

Mix one cup self-rising flour, one cup sugar, and one cup 2% or whole milk with wire whisk until all lumps are gone and it is smooth! Pour this batter over the melted butter and DO NOT STIR! Gently ladle in the peaches and simple syrup over the batter. DO NOT STIR!

Place into preheated oven. Bake 35-45 minutes (you know your oven) until cobbler is golden brown and crust has risen to the top! Serve the cobbler while warm with a scoop of vanilla ice cream on top.

WEEK 3 – The Preparation

Preparation is part of our lives from start to finish. We prepare for the birth of a baby. We prepare for that baby to start school, go to college, and get married. We prepare our finances so that we have money set aside for emergencies. Preparation for retirement, old age, and death are some of the less-than-fun preparations that must be made. Life is full of opportunities to prepare for what lies around the corner.

Jesus was in the preparation business when He came to earth. His sole purpose in leaving heaven and taking on humanity was to provide a way for you and me to be prepared for eternity. He never turned back from His preparation or His assignment.

As we consider the idea of preparation, let us ponder not only an event, but also our hearts and lives.

 OUR PREPARATION

Preparing for a *Tasting Grace* event requires some forethought and planning. No matter the size of your group, you will need to know the number of attendees in order to purchase the right amount of ingredients for your recipes.

Jan hosts a larger group than I because she utilizes her church kitchen for her event, while my event is in my home. You will want to keep your group small enough that everyone can participate in some or all aspects of the food preparation.

It is inevitable that a few ladies will sign up for the event and then need to cancel. Be sure and plan for this when you set your registration numbers.

A few days before the event, make a list of all the ingredients that you will need to prepare the dishes. In addition, make another list that includes pots, pans, utensils, dishes, and anything else that you will need. Don't forget about the items that are needed for your group to taste their creations, and if appropriate, to take a sample of their creation home. Make sure you have something for the ladies to sip on while they are working in the kitchen.

Do your grocery shopping for the event one or two days prior to the event. Shopping further out than two days puts you in the position of ending up with too many supplies should any ladies cancel. A few days before the event, you might want to print out copies of the recipes that you will prepare at the event for your attendees to take home with them.

On the day prior to the event, set up your kitchen so that everything is within reach. We encourage you to pray over your kitchen, as well as each lady, before they arrive. Ask the Lord to help you serve and minister to all who will attend.

YOUR TOOLS – DEVOTIONALS

#1 - The Bread of Life – John 6:32-51

I am the bread of life. Whoever comes to me will never go hungry, and whoever believes in me will never be thirsty. John 6:35

Some thoughts from Jan:

> As I sit here typing right now, my stomach is growling…loud enough to be heard, but thankfully I'm alone. I'm hungry, or better yet, *hangry,* a sort of new word that means you're hungry and angry about being hungry. You see, my doctor's office changed my appointment time from early morning to mid-afternoon for my yearly physical. I'm fasting, which is a requirement for accurate lab results. I haven't eaten a bite since supper last night and right now it's 2:20 in the afternoon, so I'm going on almost 24 hours without food. Yep, I'm hangry. Quite hangry.

The harsh reality is that hunger is very real to millions of people who go to bed each night with stomachs growling. One mission's conference several years ago focused on hunger. The advertising material used to encourage the attendees to think about world hunger included the tag line, *"Empty bellies have no ears."* The message was the importance of meeting physical needs *and* spiritual needs. The thought of hungry children should be a hard thing for our hearts and minds to ponder. Many children around the world never have the blessing of experiencing a bedtime snack of milk and cookies.

Physical starvation is cruel. It has been said that even those in wartime concentration camps spoke more often of food than freedom. Spiritual starvation is equally cruel.

There is a food for your soul that can conquer spiritual hunger…the hunger that can cry louder than any growling stomach. It is found in Christ alone. Only Jesus can fully satisfy that longing of the heart. Not religion or philosophy or success or money. Jesus Christ, the Bread of Life, is the only thing that will satiate spiritual hunger. He came to give His life so that we may live forever in Heaven with God. And not only that we may live forever, but also that we may be victorious day to day with all the mess that life throws at us. When we embrace Jesus we will experience the true satisfaction that He alone can give.

So today, ask Him to satisfy the longings of your soul. Ask Him to fill you to the brim with His love and grace. Thank Him that He is the true Bread of Life, the daily bread that brings life-changing nourishment.

#2 – Don't Stir Up Trouble – Proverbs 6:19

Often in today's world we hear people talk about how God is a God of love—and He is very much that. God's love is so vast and immeasurable that it is impossible to completely comprehend it. We must, however, be sure that we understand all of God's character. He is not only a God of love, but He is also a God of justice and righteousness. It is impossible to have one without the other…love and justice.

Because God is a God of righteousness and justice, there are some things that He will not tolerate. In fact, there are some things that He flat out hates.

Read Proverbs 6:16-19:

There are six things the LORD hates, seven that are detestable to him:
1. *haughty eyes*
2. *a lying tongue*
3. *hands that shed innocent blood*
4. *a heart that devises wicked schemes*
5. *feet that are quick to rush into evil*
6. *a false witness who pours out lies*
7. *a man who stirs up dissension among brothers*

Verse 19 addresses causing conflict among family members. It is important to remember that this can be our physical family, whatever that looks like, or our spiritual family.

Let's consider how we might stir up dissension or cause conflict in the family. There are obvious ways that it can be done such as picking a fight or being rude and ugly to another family member. It could also happen because of poor communication between family members.

Let's consider some not-so-obvious ways to be a troublemaker. How about discontentment? Satan loves to make us discontent with our life situations. When that happens, we begin to look for alternatives. Sometimes discontent serves as a catalyst toward positive, God-ordained change. Other times, however, discontentment breeds contempt within a family, and that may cause trouble and fighting.

Jealousy is another way to cause conflict within a family. It can be jealousy over a family member's possessions or jealousy over family relationships. All too often, parents favor one child over another, treating one differently than the other or giving one child more than another. This is a sure way to cause trouble in a family.

How about a critical spirit? That will light up the fires of dissension faster than lighter fluid on wood. When one person criticizes another, walls are built and relationships are destroyed.

Gossip is another source of trouble and conflict within families. We must be careful about the things we share that concern another person. If we have not been asked to repeat the information, we must not share it with anyone else.

Lying and deception cause conflict. Any time one person tries to deceive another person, there is sure to be trouble. Trust is broken, and family relationships can be permanently damaged by lying and deception.

So, how do we keep from being one who stirs up dissension among brothers?

First, ask God to keep you from being one who stirs up trouble. This is a prayer that God will absolutely answer. Ask Him to show you anything in your heart that might cause you to be a troublemaker.

Second, be very careful with your words. The spoken word can never be unspoken. Our words have power to heal or hurt. The hurt and trouble that result from a carelessly or vindictively spoken word can last a lifetime.

Third, treat other people as you would want to be treated. Do you want someone stirring up trouble for you? Of course not. So, do not be causing trouble for someone else. It is your choice. Do you look like the devil or like Jesus to other people?

You and I should strive to be peacemakers, not troublemakers.

RECIPES FOR WEEK 3

#1 – Chocolate Cobbler

6 tablespoons butter

1 cup self-rising flour

¾ cup white sugar

1 ½ tablespoons unsweetened cocoa powder

½ cup milk

1 teaspoon vanilla extract

1 cup white sugar

¼ cup unsweetened cocoa powder

1 ½ cups boiling water

Preheat oven to 350° F. Melt butter in an 8" x 8" baking dish in the oven while it preheats.

Directions:
In a medium bowl, stir together flour, ¾ cup sugar, and 1 ½ tablespoon cocoa. Stir in milk and vanilla until smooth. Spoon this batter over the melted butter in the baking dish. Stir together the remaining 1-cup of sugar and ¼ cup cocoa powder. Sprinkle over batter. Pour boiling water over the top of the mixture. Bake until set for 30-35 minutes in the preheated oven. The crust will rise to the top. The cobbler is wonderful as is, or it can be served while still warm with a scoop of vanilla ice cream on top.

#2 - Grandma Eula's Homemade Chicken and Dumplings

1 chicken, stewed and deboned with some of the skin remaining

1 quart or larger chicken broth

2 cups self-rising flour

¼ cup lard or Crisco® shortening

Buttermilk—approximately ⅔ - ¾ cup

One stick REAL butter

1 TBSP salt

1 TBSP black pepper

Directions:

To be honest, these amounts are negotiable. Grandma Colwell did not give amounts in her recipe, and so I just guess about everything. These are really easy, I promise.

Stew the chicken in large pot of water and/or chicken broth for 1 hour. Cool until you can handle comfortably. Pull the meat off the bone, placing half of it back in the pot with the liquid, and discard bone. Keep the other half to add back in after your dumplings are cooked.

Make very firm dumpling dough, using biscuit recipe from Week 1. You will use a bit less buttermilk for dumplings than you do for biscuits. Allow the dough to rise in a warm place for up to 2 hours. Bring chicken and broth to boil. Add in butter, salt and pepper. Knead dough a couple of times on a floured surface and roll out very, very thin, using a rolling pin. I usually roll out my dough in two batches.

With a blunt knife, cut strips of dumplings. I cut mine about 1 inch wide and 2-3 inches long. Do whatever suits you. Drop dumplings into boiling pot a few at a time, allowing some of the flour from the surface where you rolled out the dough to go into the pot along with the dough. The flour helps the liquid thicken.

Once the first batch of dough is in the pot, turn the heat down to low, cover the pot, and allow it to cook while you roll out and cut the second batch of dough.

Turn the heat back to high and drop the second batch of dumplings in the pot. Make sure you stir gently between batches so the chicken doesn't stick to the bottom of the pan. After the second batch of dumplings is in the pot, turn the heat to medium, replace the lid on the pot, and allow it to cook for about 10 minutes. Turn off the heat and let the dumplings sit until you are ready to eat.

I usually make my chicken and dumplings up to two hours before we want to eat them. This allows the liquid to thicken up a bit. I don't rewarm them before serving, but you could. Enjoy and know my Grandma Colwell is smiling on you!

WEEK 4 – The Event

In just a few moments your ladies will be sitting before you, eager to learn how to try some new recipes. You have prayed, planned, and prepared, and God will honor your efforts.

As the ladies arrive, greet them and give them a nametag if the group does not know each other. Offer them something to sip on while they wait. Jan and I have our devotional time at the beginning of the session. It lasts for no more than 10 minutes. You may choose to do yours at the end while they all taste their creations.

Be sure to get a picture of your group sometime during the event and send them to us. We want to see the beautiful faces of the ladies who attend.

It is time to begin! Relax and enjoy your event. It will be a blessing to everyone who attends!

 OUR EVENTS

After my (Leah's) first *Tasting Grace* event where I taught a group of four ladies to make homemade biscuits, one of the ladies sent me a message that really highlights the goal for the *Tasting Grace* event. She said: "I was super blessed today! Many days I feel inadequate as a mom and baking fears add to that. I now feel empowered!"

I have had other ladies send me pictures showing the dishes they made in their own kitchens after being at the event. *Tasting Grace* not only teaches them how to make a dish, it gives them the confidence to go into their own kitchen and do it.

Jan and I believe with our whole hearts that God delights over each *Tasting Grace* event. Why? Because we are being obedient to do what the apostle Paul told us to do as older women. Obedience brings blessing!

 YOUR TOOLS – DEVOTIONALS

#1 – Oaks, Acorns and Legacies

"Great people plant shade trees they'll never sit under." —Alfred North Whitehead
Did you know that tree planting and legacy building have much in common? Think about the quote you just read. Whitehead knew a lot about legacy.

Every moment of every day you and I are building our legacy. We are systematically, whether intentionally or unintentionally, creating the picture of our lives with our thoughts, words, and actions.

Today, let's consider our legacy in light of tree planting.

Suppose I hopped in my car and drove to a local nursery. I tell the nursery manager I would like to plant some oak seedlings so that I could have some shade on my house from the afternoon sun. I go on to tell him that the oak will have to be pretty tall to give me that shade because I have a two-story home. While I am speaking, I notice that his brow is elevating, and his face gives away the fact that he is about to tell me something I don't necessarily want to hear.

Mr. Manager says to me, *"Ma'am, it takes an oak tree approximately 80 years to grow to full maturity. If you plant a seedling today, you probably will not live to see it give you the kind of shade you are seeking. One day, it will be a mighty fine shade tree, but not in your lifetime."*

So it is with our lives and legacies. Many of the words we speak and the things we do today will not bear fruit in our lifetime. Do them anyway! Some of the greatest moments of our legacy will be those words and deeds planted in the lives of others that bear fruit long after we move into heaven.

How do we plant trees and build legacies from which others can benefit? Consider seven tips:

1. **Accept Jesus as your Lord and Savior.** That is where a godly legacy begins.

2. **Actively cultivate your relationship with Jesus through prayer and study of the Scriptures.**

3. **Ask the Lord to help you live a life that leaves a godly legacy.** The Holy Spirit will help you live a life that exhibits a godly character and holiness before a world that desperately needs to see those things.

4. **Give your life away. Serve others sacrificially.** Make Romans 12:1 a reality in your life. *Therefore, I urge you, brothers, in view of God's mercy, to offer your bodies as living sacrifices, holy and pleasing to God—this is your spiritual act of worship.*

5. **Seek ways to build relationships with younger people (both chronologically and spiritually) so you can speak the truth of Jesus into their lives.** Mentoring is a wonderful way to speak godly truth into the next generation.

6. **Decide today that you will be submissive and obedient to whatever the Lord asks you to do.** God has promised to bless those who bend their knee to His will. Consider 1 Samuel 15:22. *But Samuel replied: Does the LORD delight in burnt offerings and sacrifices as much as in obeying the voice of the LORD? To obey is better than sacrifice, and to heed is better than the fat of rams.*

7. **Keep your eyes fixed on Jesus.** This may be redundant, but it is so, so important. Satan will try to lure your eyes to other things. Don't let him. Hebrews 12:2 reminds us to, *Let us fix our eyes on Jesus, the author and perfecter of our faith, who for the joy set before him endured the cross, scorning its shame, and sat down at the right hand of the throne of God.*

Focusing on these seven legacy-building tips will ensure that you plant mighty oaks under which many generations will sit.

#2 – Psalm 131:1-2 – Choosing Peace

O Lord, my heart is not lifted up; my eyes are not raised too high; I do not occupy myself with things too great and too marvelous for me. But I have calmed and quieted my soul, like a weaned child with its mother; like a weaned child is my soul within me.

Read the beginning of verse 2 to your group once more. *But I have calmed and quieted my soul.*

We live in a busy, hurried, and harried world. We say "yes" more often than we say "no". We forfeit family time for a multitude of other, seemingly good, things. We push and pull and tug; we fight and scratch and kick so we can make it to the top rung of whatever ladder we are climbing. And we wonder why we have no peace in our hearts.

In John 14:27 Jesus told His followers that He was the source of peace, and He would give it to them. He did. He will. He does. Yet, Psalm 131:2 reminds us that in order to have that peace, there is something we must do.

You and I must make a choice to calm and quiet our souls. It is not an easy choice in the world in which we live, and that choice will look different for each of us. We may need to:

- Carve out time for Bible study and prayer
- Say "No" to more activity
- Find an accountability partner
- Take a vacation or sabbatical
- Turn off mobile devices and social media
- Take a hike or a drive and enjoy the beauty of nature

Whatever is required to calm and quiet our souls is what we need to be intentional about doing. Our peace depends on it. Our intimacy with Jesus depends on it. Our family relationships depend on it.

Enter into a short time of discussion with your group. Ask the following questions of them.

- *Do you feel like your soul is hurried and busy or quieted and peaceful the majority of the time?*

- *Are you intentional about seeking peace through calming and quieting your soul?*

- *What would it take for you to calm and quiet your soul?*

#1 – Gran Jan's Cornbread Recipe

1 ½ cups White Lily self-rising buttermilk cornmeal

½ cup of White Lily self-rising flour

1 egg

1 ½ cups buttermilk

¼ cup oil

Crisco or Lard (to grease skillet)

Directions:
Preheat oven to 450°. Mix oil and egg, add buttermilk, and then cornmeal and flour. Mix the wet and dry ingredients well. Generously grease a cast-iron skillet with Crisco. Sprinkle dry cornmeal over the Crisco in the pan. Pour the cornbread mixture in the skillet. Bake 20-25 minutes until nicely browned.

Notes:

_____

_____

_____

_____

_____

_____

_____

_____

_____

_____

#2 – Jan's Cornbread Dressing

*Cornbread dressing is a staple of Southern Thanksgiving tables. Here is a basic recipe with variations included at the end. Experiment and discover what your family loves and make it your own! Basically, **Southern Cornbread Dressing** is comprised of good broth and a mixture of ⅔ cornbread and ⅓ white bread (or biscuits or even saltine crackers). You can buy canned broth, but if you'll take time and make your own broth it is the best! If possible, put the dressing together the day before you intend to bake it in order to allow time for the flavors to meld.* **MAKES 9" x 13" PAN**

1 pan of cornbread, crumbled – about 7-8 cups (see cornbread recipe)

White bread or biscuits (allowed to dry out), crumbled – about 3 cups (OR ½ sleeve crushed saltines).

Salt and black pepper to taste

2 tsp. poultry seasoning (optional)

3 eggs, beaten

1 stick butter (softened) to sauté celery and onion

1 ½ cups celery and 1 large onion [or to taste] (chop fine and sauté in butter until soft)

1 can herbed cream of chicken soup (or plain cream of chicken soup)

Chicken stock/broth (BOIL 2 ½ quarts of water, salt, pepper, 3-4 chicken thighs or if you are roasting a turkey, you may use the turkey neck, ½ stick of butter, 2 chopped onions, 2-3 stalks of celery-include leaves.) [You won't use ALL the broth, but you can freeze to use later as soup base.]

Preheat oven to 400° F.

Directions:
Grease 9" x 13" pan. In a large bowl, crumble cornbread and dried white bread slices (or saltines, biscuits). Melt butter in a large skillet over medium heat and add chopped celery and onion. Cook until transparent, about 5 to 10 minutes. Pour celery and onion mixture over the cornbread mixture.

Strain your chicken stock and pour hot broth over cornbread and mix well. You want the dressing to be the consistency of oatmeal, not too soupy, not too thick. **TASTE NOW BEFORE ADDING EGGS!** Add salt & pepper to taste (and sage or poultry seasoning if you use them—LESS IS MORE!)

Add 3 beaten eggs and mix well. Pour into greased casserole pan and bake at 400°- 425° until browned on top, about 30-45 minutes.

Continued on next page.

VARIATIONS:

- A small jar of chopped pimentos for color, be sure to drain first
- Bag of Pepperidge Farm Herb Stuffing for more herbed flavor
- Poultry Seasoning (to taste)
- Sage seasoning (to taste)
- Canned chicken broth instead of homemade
- Leave out celery
- Add cooked chopped turkey or chicken to the dressing prior to baking

Notes:

_____

_____

_____

_____

_____

_____

#2- Layered Mexican Chicken Salad

1 cup ranch dressing

2 tsp taco seasoning mix

4 cups Romaine or other lettuce, torn or shredded

1 can black beans, or other bean of choice, drained

1 can whole kernel corn, drained

1 small onion, chopped

1 bell pepper, color of choice, chopped

Meat of 1 deli rotisserie chicken, chopped

1 - 2 cups Hint-o-Lime tortilla chips or other lime- flavored tortilla chips, crushed coarsely

1 cup shredded Mexican-style cheese

¾ cup grape or cherry tomatoes

Directions:
Mix dressing with taco seasoning. Set aside. Layer lettuce through cheese in order in a large dish. Drizzle with dressing. Place tomatoes on top as garnish.

G od's grace is boundless, bottomless, and never-ending! His grace is one of the most bountiful of blessings in the life of a follower of Jesus Christ. Hopefully, you have grown more confident in the kitchen now and have a deeper understanding of God's word too!

A Tasting Grace event is really simple at its best and is what makes this mentoring so refreshing. Just be yourself, and share your love for Jesus and for cooking at the same time! So as a next step, consider hosting your own Tasting Grace ministry in your community, home, or church, and pass on your newfound knowledge.

When you partner up with a friend and start your own group, you will continue to learn and grow as you teach others! This ministry reaches through to families and homes. Never forget that God's grace is limitless, and so are the ideas and possibilities for this fun-filled way to mentor in the kitchen.

Our grandmothers would be so proud of how their granddaughters have carried on their legacies with Tasting Grace.

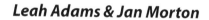

Leah Adams & Jan Morton

Notes: